Octave Thanet

A book of true lovers

Octave Thanet

A book of true lovers

ISBN/EAN: 9783742891525

Manufactured in Europe, USA, Canada, Australia, Japa

Cover: Foto ©Thomas Meinert / pixelio.de

Manufactured and distributed by brebook publishing software
(www.brebook.com)

Octave Thanet

A book of true lovers

A BOOK OF TRUE LOVERS

By OCTAVE THANET

NEW YORK. DOUBLEDAY & McCLURE CO. 1899

Note

——

"The Strike at Glasscock's" was first
published in the *Northwestern Miller*, "The
Judgment on Mrs. Swift" and "The Court
of Last Resort," in *Peterson's Magazine*
(1893), "The Dilemma of Sir Guy the
Neuter," in *Scribner's Magazine*, "The
Ladder of Grief," in *McClure's Magazine*,
"Why Abbylonia Surrendered," in *Harper's Bazar*, and "The Captured Dream,"
in *Harper's Magazine*.

Nothing is sweeter than Love, nothing
stronger, nothing higher,
Nothing wider, nothing more pleasant,
Nothing fuller or better
In heaven or on earth.
　　　　　　　　—Thomas a Kempis.

To the Gentle Reader

Mine Unknown but Dearly Esteemed Friend:

It hath been a pleasure for me to gather into this little volume a few stories regarding the joys and sorrows, the adventures and misadventures of divers true lovers whom I have known, trusting that such may be of profit and entertainment.

The lovers in the first tale, albeit of small pretense to sentiment or to daintiness of living, were, none the less, of assured faithfulness, and fond of each other in their mute fashion. The hero of the old world tale that followeth, did prefer his honor to friendship and the strong movings of compassion and even to love itself, yet seemeth to me, nevertheless, a true lover. In the Judgment on Mistress Swift are two lovers, one of whom was always true, and the other found love only through grief and shame, seeing first the false love, before her soul recognized the true. While Abbylonia, as the speech of the vulgar runneth, "didn't know when she was well off," and mistook true love for the feeble counterfeit that fails under the trials of a common journey into the world; yet for her is great excuse, since there is no lonelier lot, nor one fuller of gallsome toil and privation, than that of the farmer's wife. There is no excuse for the weak creature whose faithful wife appealed to the court of last resort, but since she was satisfied with her sorry bargain he is admitted to the company. Whatever his faults, the man whose grief became the ladder whereon he climbed to a higher and more unselfish love, was a true lover. And the old couple in " The Captured Dream " were the truest lovers of all. If, my dear friend, you perceive that the love herein depicted deals more with married folks than with youths and maidens, may I humbly suggest that as we should call no man happy until he be dead, so likewise may we hesitate to call a lover true until he hath been proved by marriage, which is as a fire or an ireful acid, releasing all the volatile and unsubstantial elements of love, and leaving only the pure gold of the heart.

That so much of it remains in the marriages of our Anglo-Saxon race is the happiest omen for us as a people.

Having thus sketched the lovers in each tale, it is for you to choose which you may care to read, and for me to wish you all happiness in your own loves, present and to come.

I am your most obedient, humble servant,

THE AUTHOR.

Contents

		PAGE
THE STRIKE AT GLASSCOCK'S	.	1
THE JUDGMENT ON MRS. SWIFT	.	23
THE DILEMMA OF SIR GUY THE NEUTER		77
THE COURT OF LAST RESORT	.	143
WHY ABBYLONIA SURRENDERED	.	169
THE LADDER OF GRIEF	. . .	219
THE CAPTURED DREAM	. . .	259

The Strike at Glasscock's

The Strike at Glasscock's.

❧

'Tis in vain to kick when a man is once fettered.—*Montaigne.*

"IF you call these arrangements primitive," said my friend, the colonel, flashing his white teeth through the lint-dusted atmosphere of the cotton gin, and, with one sweep of the arm, indicating the three chambers of the mill — cotton gin, lumber mill and grist mill — "if you are moved to your very unnecessary and impolite mirth by such little trifles as engines running without a fence around them, I wish you could have seen a mill I saw last week." Then, being properly importuned, he told me about it.

"I was riding through the bottom, after some timber I wanted to look at, with a view to selling, and somehow I lost my way. I came out on a new clearing. I never had seen it before, or the fence about the thrifty garden, or the house of lumber, built tight,

1

and three-fourths painted, with a man on a
ladder, slapping the yellow paint on the
battened walls; or the shed of a mill on the
river bank, under a great water oak.   Not
a wisp of smoke drifted out of the rusty
stovepipe that was the mill chimney. There
wasn't a sound, either, except the calls of
the birds and the cheeping of a crowd of
chickens in the front yard.

"I hailed the man, and he got his neck
and one shoulder around far enough to stare
at me.

"'That a mill?' says I.

"'Used to be, yesterday,' says he.

"'Sell me some meal for my horse?'

"'No, sir.   All out, and ain't runnin'.'

"'What's the matter?'

"'Crew on a strike.'

"'What's the matter with *them?*'

"The man deliberately hooked his pail
over the ladder, and leisurely descended.
He was a long, gaunt old fellow, well griz-
zled, and his tough old face was scored with
a network of wrinkles. His gray beard had
a close curl to it, as had his silky gray hair,
and his blue eyes twinkled in a half shrewd,

half humorous way that was rather prepossessing. He was clean, too, which is a distinction in some parts of this country. 'Obstinate as the devil,' I said to myself, 'but most likely honest, and knows a joke when he sees one.' I knew he was fixing to tell me the whole story the minute he swung off from the ladder.

"'Set down,' said he; 'mought as well res' you' hoss a spell; hot day to-day, and mussiful man 's mussiful to his beastis, ye know. Have drink er muscadine cider?'

"He brought a drink that came out of a stone jug slung in the well, and tasted cool and pleasant. In return I handed him a cigar; and we were at once on most amicable terms. 'Yes,' he resumed, '*'tis* kinder embarrassin', Saturday comin' on to-morrer, and most like folks comin' round fer meal, to be fixed this here way; an' I tole the widder so, but thar warn't no movin' of her.'

"'The widow?'

"'Yes, sir'—he had one of the soft, slurring voices that you don't hear out of the south, voices that linger on the vowels,

and let the consonants get along by themselves; for my part I like to hear our people
talk, just for the sound of it—'yes, sir, the
widder, my wife.   Nice a woman as you 'll
ever meet up with, and good a cook, tew,
but the Lord made most wimmen fools, and
all on 'em stubborn.   And once git her set,
thar ain't no movin' of the widder.   So here
I be, with nothin' but my own cookin' to
depend on, an' mill shut down.'

"'You mean your wife and you have
parted?' said I, using the common expression of the country.

"'Parted be d——d!' bawled he, firing
instantly, 'parted nothin'! Didn't I tell you
she ben on the strike?'

"'And your mill crew also?'

"'Well, stranger,' was his sardonic comment, 'you don't look nigh as dumb as ye
be.   Bless ye, *she* air the crew!'

"'The mill crew?'

"'Yes, sir, the plumb crew; how much
of a crew do you expect?'

"'Aren't you a little short-handed?'

"'Course we ain't.   Come down to that
mill and I 'll show you.   We got a daisy en-

gine, peart as ye cud ask. I run the saw when we air a-sawin', and she pumps the bar'l full er water; and we got a inspirator to draw it into the en*gine*, and when we use that up we stop and fire her up agin. She pumps the water and chops up the slabs that I saw off fur the en*gine*, and I run the saw or the grist. Every feller that comes dips his own sack full out of the box and feeds the huller, tew; so we don't have nare trouble. We *didn't* — tell she struck.'

"'Why did she strike?'

"'Well, it warn't fur wages, ezackly, nor it warn't agin the union — natchelly not, seein' we air the union ourselves. What ruined our fambly is just cravin' fur style and show, and the natchell yearnin' of wimmen to have their own way. We'd of been married thirty-three year come next September, and we hain't never had no 'casion fer havin' a house paintid, when she got it inter her head, or Susan Ma'y put it thar, that she wanted a paintid house. She tole me of a Sunday that she'd ben dwellin' on the idee fur a right smart.

"'"Ye best ondwell, then," says I.

"Paint air onhealthy, and I don't want none er it in mine." "Tain't neither," says she; "the cholera is comin', and the doctors say paint—fresh paint—is a perventatative," says she, terrible uppish. But it warn't no perventatative she ben ayfter. It ben fur the looks of the thing, and I knowed it. Ye see, the widder allus had a hankerin' fur fine things. We ain't got no less 'n four rockin' cheers to our house. Fact. And she won't w'ar a sunbunnit to church. Got to have a bunnit or a straw hat. An' she kinder tolled me inter paintin' an' paperin' inside tell we was so dadgummed fine she cudn't have my old dog inside in muddy weather. 'Clare, *that* made me mad. An' what made me madder, she had to git a stove in the room, an' I hadn't nare place on earth to spit in 'cept a box! What do you reckon 'bout that? Air that the way to treat a self-respectin' citizen with a white skin—makin' of him spit in a *box?* Oh, it air all Susy Ma'y, her daughter—*I* knows her. She married a man ain't got no no- tions 'cept to please her! Dretful fool 's ye ever did see! Makes a heap er money runnin' a mill, an' got a house fur her made outer a book. Yes, sir, I seen it in the book. Gits things fur his mill outer a book, tew. Has high 's fifteen men foolin' with that mill, an' lumber ain't planed a bit better 'n mine. Got a cotton gin on it, and grinds cotton, tew.'

"It was plain his disapproval of his son-in-law struggled with pride in his possessions; but I had seen that sort of thing before, and I knew enough to keep my mouth shut. He went on describing the glories of Susan Ma'y's house and yard. She had a carpet with roses on it, and china vases, and a clock, and a gold watch, and curtains in the windows, and lamps with white shades over the chimneys made it light as day all night. 'And she puts the widder up to all manner er nonsense,' he concluded, ferociously.

"'That's your step-daughter, I suppose,' said I, to keep the conversation brisk, and get the old man in the humor to let me get some meal, somehow, for my horse. The poor beast had the lampers, and needed soft food.

" 'Step-daughter!' said he, sharply; 'no, she ain't; widder an' me ain't never ben married, 'cept to each other.'

" 'Oh, it was only from her being called Mrs.—your wife's daughter, and you calling your wife the widow,' I hazarded.

" ' That 's 'cause she favors her maw, an' ain't got nare sense like me,' he snarled back. 'Ain't you never heard married folks talk afore? An' I calls her the widder, 'cause if I was to die she wud be the widder Glasscock, wudn't she? She 'd stay so, too! An' she mought ez well begin to hear it. We ain't got nare nother child nor Susan Ma'y, neither. Now you got us straight in you' mind, stranger?'

" 'I reckon,' said I.

" 'Well, so ye have, I kin go on to the p'int. We kep' at it. She ben wantin' of me to take a paper, "so we 'll know the news," says she. I says, "We ain't no need er news, 'cept what we kin git oncet a month, at preachin'," but I says, when this come up, "If I 'll git ye a paper oncet a week will ye quit bellerin' at me?" Says she, "I dunno how to b'ar hit without we

git the house paintid." "Ye cayn't have
the house paintid," says I, "but I'll git ye
the paper." And I done got her the paper.
And she read it to me reg'lar. She kin
read the best in the world, right off; nev'
does have to stop an' spell, not even to
whisper words off to herseff. An' she use
to read all 'bout them strikes an' sich —
reckon ye know on 'em?'

"'I've heard,' said I.

"'Kinder fool things, to my notion, but
she got dredful struck by 'em. An' she
kep' at me 'bout the paint—axed me twicet
in one week—"say, squire, ain't you goin'
to paint?"—jest like that, mighty fine an'
mincin'. "No, I ain't," says I; "you quit
you' foolin' 'bout paint or I'll quit *you!*" —
jest like that, awful stern an' determined.
I 'lowed it wud shet her up. Sayd it to her
twicet. Fust time she didn't say nary, jest
taken a bite on her snuff stick, an' santered
off. Nex' time she says, right low an'
pleasant, "Say, squire, if I was to pay fur
the paint wud it make ary differ in you'
feelin's?" "You ain't got nare money,"
says I, fur I knowed she done spent ever'

last cent she got from her chickens on a colt she bought fur me ter go ridin'.' His countenance wore the queerest expression over the last sentence; I believe he wanted to convey to me, without telling, that his rebellious wife really did, as we call it down here, set a heap of store by him. He went on, scraping the dried paint off the palms of his hands as he talked, with his finger nails. ' " You ain't got nare money." I sayd that. " How come ye cayn't let me work it out at the mill?" says she. " I isn't to pay you fur workin' to the mill," says I; "I never did pay ye one cent." " Time ye begun, then," says she, "fur I don't 'low to strike nary nuther lick ter the mill tell ye gives me you' word 'bout that ar paint." " Oh, you' goin' to strike, be ye?" says I. "All right fur you." And I went home, mad. I cudn't someway b'ar to be beat by her cussedness, and I kep' a-turnin' an' a-turnin' it over, an' studyin' 'bout it, an' I reckon I got madder an' madder, fur to tell ye the bones' truth, stranger, I ben fixin' ter give in to that ar fool woman, seein' how she did work so good ever' other way; an' fact is, I had

bought that ar paint to the store—leastways
I had priced it—an' I 'lowed if she begged
right hard I cud ride over an' git it, nex'
mornin', mud not bein' more 'n shoe-mouth
deep, nowhar, an' road good. So, natchelly,
that made me all the madder, me meanin'
so well by her, an' her cuttin' up rough that
way, an' doin' me so mean! So—we was
out to the paschure—we all got a right fine
paschure an' some mighty nice cows—an'
she ben a milkin' when I named the matter
to her—so I jest lit out an' leff her a-milk-
in'. Didn't offer to holp tote the pails or
nothin'; jest went a-streakin' back with my
mad up! Say, stranger, you married?'

"I said I was so fortunate.

"'Well, then,' and he rolled the scrap-
ings of paint into a ball in the hollow of his
palms, and gave a sigh of relief, 'then you
know thar ain't nare nother critter on earth
kin make ye mad as you' wife; an' looks
like the more ye think on her, the madder
she kin rile ye. I ben that mad I cudn't
see straight; an' when, as I turned away,
all choked up, I heerd the swish, splash of
the milk drappin' into the pail, steady like,

an' knowed she hadn't turned a h'ar fur
all my r'arin' an' chargin'—looked like I
wanted to spite her wuss 'n I ever did want
anythin'! But I turns 'round, an' I sayd,
"Mistress Glasscock," says I, "to-morrer
is Saturday, an' thar is like to be ten men,
maybe, 'long here to have their corn ground.
Do you mean to tell me ye won't holp me
with them men a-grindin'?" "I mean I
done struck," says she, "like them men
you read on. You knows on what terms
I'll come back—the house prommussed to
be paintid." An' she went at the cow agin,
swish, splash. "All right fur you!" says I.
And I never *did* turn my head on her agin,
but I walked right spang home, and I went
in, an' I nailed a bar agin all three er the
doors, an' then I got the kettle an' the coffee
pot on the stove, an' went out an' cut some
meat an' got it a-sizzlin', an' I sot down.
D'reckly I heerd her a-comin'. Then she
tried the door. We didn't have nare locks
nur bolts on the doors, an' I 'lowed she mis-
trustid; but I set dumb 's a wil' hog when
ye stick him. One by one, she tried ever'
last door. Then she spoke. "What is you

aimin' to do, Sam Glasscock?" says she, kinder flustered like; an' I answered back, "You' mighty sharp, Mistress Glasscock, but you cayn't cut *me*. I read the papers, tew. If you' a-strikin', I 'm a-lockin' ye out. That ar 's what I air aimin' at, Mistress Glasscock!"'

"He paused to let me appreciate the impressiveness of his retort, and flung the little ball of paint at a hen that had strayed into the garden and was nibbling at the rows of peas.

"'What did she say,' said I.

"He sighed heavily, and said: 'She jest kinder laughed, right spiteful like, an', ayfter a plumb minnit, endurin' wich she hadn't made nare sound er rattlin' the winders, nur poundin' on the doors, nur nary, an' I ben kinder coolin' off, she sayd: "Sam, if ye want to fix it that a way, you kin; but when ye want me back, remember I ain't a-comin', less 'n to a paintid house." She nev' *did* say nuthin' more. I waited on her to speak, cause I ben gettin' more an' more cooled off, but I didn't hear nuthin', an' bymeby, when I come to look out '—he got up, frowned and shook himself as a dog will, you know, before he concluded—'well, that's all; she were plumb gone!'

"Somehow, for all his bravado, I guessed that it had hurt him.

"In a moment or two, he went on his plaint, with his back to me: 'We all ben man an' wife fur thirty-three year, an' we ain't never *did* ben apart a night before; an' it ben ever' mite her fault, I tole myself. But I reckon I hadn't orter locked her out. Hay, stranger?'

"'I reckon you would have done better to have let her in and talked it over peaceably,' said I.

"'You reckon I best paintid the house fer her?' It was comical, the way he flung those sentences over his shoulder at me, never once turning around.

"'Can you afford it?'

"'Course I kin.'

"'Hasn't she been a good wife to you, every other way?'

"'Ain't I done tole ye that? Nobody in this yere kentry has got a better woman than me.'

"Still he kept his broad back to me; but his shoulder wriggled at each question.

"'You 'd better give in, then,' said I.

"He exploded in a second, flung himself round on me, swinging his fists and snorting, swelling like an enraged hen.

"'Give in,' he screamed, 'you bet I won't give in! I ain't that kind er man — *I* ain't! Why, look a here, I fund out better 'n that by the papers. Ain't she struck?'

"'Surely,' said I.

"'Ain't I done locked her out?'

"'So it appears,' said I.

"'Well,' triumphantly he spread his hands apart, glistening with paint, 'what do they do in the papers in these yere contests atween labor an' capitil? Is labor — that 's her — goin' to give in? Not much; it ain't got the sense! Is capitil — that 's me — goin' to lay down? Never!' — he slapped his painted jeans with a sounding thud with both hands — 'Well, how is you to manage? How does them great contestin' pyarties manage? Why, *nobuddy* gives in. They finds somebody they kin have confidence in, an' they leaves it to him, an' both on 'em will abide by his decidin'.'

"'I see,' said I gravely, 'and I ——— '

"' You air the arbitration committee, an' don't you ferget it. You decide fur paint, paint it is!'

"I ventured to suggest that he had started on the paint before the committee decided. His foot was already on the last round of the ladder and his hand outstretched to unhook the pail; but he cast a withering glance at me. 'Stranger,' he remarked, in a low, impressive voice, 'I done lived on my own cookin' ever sence last Friday week; an' does you reely reckon I air goin' to monkey round yere waitin' on a arbitration committee an' doin' nuthin'? No, sir. I knowed aforehand what a decent arbitrationer wud say, an', w'ilst I ben waitin' fur one to come by, I jest laid the paint on lively. It 'll be all on afore sundown, this evenin,' an' I kin git to Susan Ma'y, my daughter's, afore long; an' the widder has jest natchelly *got* to submit to the arbitrationer, tew, an' come 'long home; an' ef the fraish paint makes her plumb sick, tain't nare fault er mine! An' I never *will* paint agin.'

"So saying, he addressed himself so vigorously to his painting that I rather felt myself in the way. However, I interrupted him long enough to inquire my road, and then I took it, since cornmeal, under the present strained relations of labor and capital at Glasscock's, seemed out of reach. I had not gone very far before I came upon what we call a hack; that is, a spring wagon drawn by a very good pair of horses, and driven by a woman much better dressed than one will often see on a country road. Beside her sat a little, wiry, meek-faced old woman in a sunbonnet. I didn't need to see them turn down the cross-road to Glasscock's, to make out that there had been some sort of an arbitration committee for the party of the second part, also.

"I lodged that night not far from the mill, and in the morning I rode back to it. The smokestack was puffing away. Outside a small figure, in a short blue gown, was swinging an ax with a most extraordinary agility. It was the crew of the mill, evidently, going to work with that zeal which is always mentioned in the newspapers after a strike ends. The mill itself, on nearer approach, turned out to be a mere shell. There was a funny little engine, and, sure enough, there were the barrel and the pump and the inspirator; and as soon as the barrel was pumped full the engine could start up. While I halted my horse and looked through one side (it had all one side open, so no doors were needed), the whistle blew and the engineer began to pump; in no time the mill started up.

"Within the grist mill there was a pile of corn on the floor, and old Glasscock was shoveling corn into the box of the sheller. The corn cobs poured out at one end and the shelled corn came in a more or less jerky stream from the middle. Glasscock, at intervals, would stop shoveling and kick the pile of corn away from the mouth of the sheller. Presently, the water barrel being emptied, the mill shut down. While the mill crew heaped slabs into the furnace the miller sifted the corn through a clumsy wire sieve and then put it into the funnel above the buhr stones. He threw off the belt from the sheller and set the grist mill going; and, as soon as the wheezing of the desultory little engine was heard, the meal began to come snowing out of the funnel below. There was a box ready to receive it, and this box he emptied into the barrel standing near.

"Noticing my horse's shadow on the floor, he glanced up. He beckoned to me to approach. 'That's her!' he said, dropping his voice and gazing with undisguised pride and satisfaction on the busy little figure; 'ain't she a terror to work? Ain't it worth arbitratin' a leetle to git sech a crew back? An' she don't put on no airs. She done begged my pardon, right humble. Wudn't mad me fur nuthin', now. Don't she keep a-movin' peart, though? Sayd she nev' *would* say paint to me agin. This yere eggsperience done humbled her shore — plumb humbled her!'

"He dwelt with such unction on the words, and she did seem so mild a creature, that I began to wonder where the victory in the present contest between labor and capital really belonged.   Wondering, I departed, although they pressed me to stay, and I began to see then a lively gratitude on the part of Mrs. Glasscock that has given me many a frying chicken since.   Just as I was leaving, old Glasscock sidled up to me. 'Say,' he muttered, 'most like you'll be goin' by the store at the cross-roads; say, tell 'em to mix me up another batch er that paint.   It'll be time fur the second coat next week!'"

The Judgment on Mrs. Swift

The Judgment on Mrs. Swift.

I.

There is nothing good nor evil save in the will.
—*Schopenhauer.*

"ONLY one omnibus?" said Mrs. Swift.

There are two omnibuses in Flowering Bridge, one pink, one blue; and they provide a striking feature for funeral processions. True enough, there was only one, the blue one, to-day. It was a pitiful little train that plodded through the whitish-gray dust past the Dagget piazza; first the omnibus, next the hearse and the single shabby landau of the village livery stable, with Marcia Wright in the corner behind her black veil and the curtain that could be pulled down—the other curtains stick fast —then half a dozen wagons and buggies filled with country people in their best clothes.

23

Mrs. Swift scanned every vehicle and every face, from the elderly features of the pall-bearers in the omnibus to Joey Pratt's freckled round cheeks in the last buggy, with a peculiar suppressed interest. With an equal interest of a different kind, Mrs. Dagget watched Mrs. Swift. She observed that, as the Pratt buggy showed its dusty back, Mrs. Swift drew a soft and tremulous sigh. One might easily take it to be a sigh of relief.

The two women sat on the front veranda of a substantial two-story house, newly painted, gray as to the weather-boarding, and vivid green as to the blinds. It was the house of the Honorable Simon Dagget, postmaster and principal storekeeper of Flowering Bridge. Mrs. Swift had come in from her farm to sell her weekly store of butter and eggs, and, according to the hospitable rural custom, she had dined with Mrs. Dagget. They sat in rocking chairs under an archway of rose bushes that dropped graceful tendrils over their heads, waiting for the hot Iowa sun to pass its meridian and permit a cooler drive home.

"I see they got the 'Piscopal minister,"
said Mrs. Swift, smoothing her skirt over
her knees. Angular knees they were, Mrs.
Swift being of a spare habit, and, moreover,
disapproving of the waste of good cloth
in frivolous draperies. Her hands were
tanned, long, and belonged to that square
type to which chirosophists ascribe a love
of order and indomitable will. They did not
wriggle at the fingers nor twitch the cloth
underneath them; having smoothed it, they
lay still, palms together, for they did not
belong to a nervous woman. They matched
the flat, broad chest and the long face, given
a square contour by cheeks sagging a little
with age. The widow Swift was a very tall
woman, not bent the fraction of an inch by
her sixty-five years or the rearing of five
boys to manhood. She had been considered
an ugly maiden and a plain young wife; but
in her silky gray hair and her widow's cap,
with her strong, bright eyes and a skin
more freshly tinted than is frequent in the
west, she was a handsome elderly woman.
Her unvarying composure lent a dignity to
her presence; whoever observed her per-

ceived that here was a nature out of the common. Her companion was stout, rosy, and, judged by rural standards, far better dressed than Mrs. Swift—who, in fact, had not altered the cut of her severe black gowns since Elder Alpheus Swift's death, twenty-six years ago—she wore a figured blue sateen frock, draped and ruffled. At the widow's speech, she rocked more vigorously.

"Well, you know Mrs. Wright, she didn't like Brother Given. I guess she never did quite forgive him for marrying Marcia to that feller. Of course, she forgave the only child she 'd got; but the minister was different. He was over in Marshalltown circuit then, and he said he didn't sense it they was a runaway couple; but she said if he didn't know, he'd oughter known! When they first come back, there was another pastor here, you know, and she went regular to church, but she never went ayfter he come."

"I guess her leaving didn't hurt," said Mrs. Swift, with a sneer. "'Twas much as she could do to hire a back pew on the side aisle, and jest half that. I did hear she

promised ten cents a Sunday, and then had
to come down to a nickel.   And lately she
wasn't there, and Marshy was talking how
she'd pay it up all to once; but she ain't
paid yit.''

"Poor thing!'' the gentler woman exclaimed; "'tain't like you, Hannah, to be
pecking at them that's down, like that.
And so liberal to the church as she used to
be! She'd have the society twice to our
once, 'cause she kept a girl the year round.
If it hadn't been my ankle is so bad, I'd have
gone to the funeral.   Hannah, you'd feel
bad if you'd been there, like I been, during
her last sickness.   I don't b'lieve they got
a cent to depend on, 'cept what Marshy gets
from her dressmaking; and that's fell off
since Mrs. Wright had to keep her bed and
there was so much tending.   But she always has got something in her hands.   Marshy's dreadful changed, Hannah.''

"Yes, lost all her beauty!   I call her real
homely now.''

"Well, I don't, then,'' cried Mrs. Dagget,
with animation; "there's something 'bout
Marshy Wright's face now that I like bet-

ter 'n I ever did.   It 's the saddest face I
know, too.   But, mercy knows, she has gone
through enough to make her look sad !   Look
at them, after all they used to have !   Why,
Hannah, it fairly made me sick to go into
the pantry, remembering the kind of pantry
Mrs. Wright used to keep—never less than
three kinds of preserves at her tea-parties
and always some pound-cake or fruit-cake
in a jar for drop-in company !   Hannah,
they didn't have so much as a tumbler of
jel.   That 's so.   Marshy come to me and
asked me if I wouldn't give her a tumbler
of my green-grape jel, 'cause her ma craved
green-grape jel, and she was sorter out of
her head toward the last, and fancied she
was well-off again, a-living in Marshy's
house, and all the pickles and things she
used to put up, standing in the pantry; and
she 'd be asking Marshy for this kind and
that kind till the poor girl didn't know which
way to turn.   I 'most cried when she says :
'If you 'll kindly let mother have the jel,
I 'll work it out afterward.'   'You poor
child,' I says, 'I guess your mother 's welcome to anything in my house, and don't

you fret; it would be a pity if, now she is back 'mong her old friends, if they can't make her comfortable.' And after that, she did let Sister Pratt and I fetch in things some.''

Mrs. Dagget stopped, out of breath, to wipe her kind eyes.

Mrs. Swift folded her arms, and in the action looked more immovable, somehow, than before. "Who'd Mis' Wright think Marshy was married to?" said she.

"Well,"—there was a flutter in Mrs. Dagget's articulation—"well, I didn't intend to name it to you, Hannah, but she thought it was—it was just Alpheus Swift, and that's the truth!"

"Now it will all come out," thought the speaker, doggedly, "and I don't know's I care. 'Tain't near so bad as what I got to say to her, anyhow. I s'pose it's my Christion duty, though. Simon says 'tis. I guess I'll jest make a break now!"

But her courage oozed out at her fingertips, which trembled over the woolen lace that she was crocheting, as Mrs. Swift deliberately creaked her chair about to face her.

"I ain't got nothing," said the firm, hard voice, "to say 'bout a dying woman's delusions. But Marshy Wright is mistaken if she thinks she 'll ever get my consent to her marrying my son. He 's got to give up her or me."

"But you were willing before, Hannah."

"If I was willing before, is no reason I should be willing now. Before, when she was engaged to Alpheus, she was the prettiest and richest girl in this county, and there wan't nothing against her 'cept being a fool, like most young girls. Now she has let her husband, that she jilted Al for, spend her money and her mother's too; and her husband 's in the penitentiary, and she ain't got a cent nor even a right to her name, for she 's divorced from him. She 's jest a sort of outcast."

"Hannah, how can you be so hard?"

"I ain't hard; I 'm just. I may as well speak out, now I 'm about it. I never was willing; I never liked them. Marshy was spoiled by going east to boarding school; she couldn't find nothing good 'nuff for her, west, ayfter that, and, naturally, when that city feller come along, that had been to college, and wore store clothes, and could make fun of us to Marshy, Al hadn't no show!" Little mottles of red had crept into Mrs. Swift's cheeks, her calm voice was deepened and roughened. Mrs. Dagget marveled over the repressed passion in her face and the unloosening of her tongue, for she was a taciturn woman. The good soul did not understand that the yeasty brooding of months was having its way. "I knew well 'nuff what it meant when Al wasn't satisfied no more to eat in the kitchen, and was everlastingly scrubbing his fingernails! Ellen Dagget, you call me hard; jest s'pose your boy, that was your baby and used to love you better 'n any critter on earth — you seen him, evening ayfter evening, slickin' himself up and going off to be poked fun at before his girl; and you seen him fooling away the money he'd worked so hard for, making her presents that was laughed at and hid away out of sight, while the city feller's books was strutting 'bout the parlor table, and flowers here and flowers there, that come by the cars, and was

wilted 'fore you'd really got the smell of
'em into your nose! Never mind, they was
all right and beautiful, 'cause they come
from him! And go on; s'pose you seen
your boy growing poorer and poorer and
paler and paler, jest wearing the flesh off
his bones with worry, and then, when she
sends him off, he won't let his own mother
say a ha'sh word about her — no, I cayn't
feel to pity her. It's a judgment."

Mrs. Dagget was watching the funeral
train; she could not decide whether it had
been joined by another buggy. She said
sorrowfully that, if Marcia Wright had
done wrong, she had certainly been punished.

"She had ought to be punished," retorted
Mrs. Swift; "it's a plain judgment on folly
and a haughty spirit."

"Well, sister," Mrs. Dagget pleaded,
mildly, "it runs in my mind always what
David says: 'If it comes to going by our
merits, oh Lord, who shall stand?' Think
of what a pretty critter she did use to be,
and every young man in the place going wild
over her; was it funny her head was turned?

Think of what she had to bear, too, him drinking and gambling and squandering her mother's money, as well as hers; yes, and spending it on such critters as he did, too! I don't blame her for getting a divorce! And, Hannah, I do say, if Marshy's sinned, she has repented, too, and tried to atone and walk humble before the Lord; and long 's He says He won't break the bruised reed, I don't feel it 's my duty to hit it a lick."

Mrs. Swift was a woman who did not value the last word; she had said what she had to say; for the rest, Mrs. Dagget might work her will on the Scriptures. She rocked in silence, with her mouth firmly closed.

After a pause, the pacific Mrs. Dagget essayed a pleasanter topic, remarking: "I heard you paid off the last on your mortgage, Hannah. I 'm real pleased."

"So am I," said Mrs. Swift, her countenance relaxing; "we have the whole of the new farm paid for now. It feels queer; we ain't been without a mortgage since Elder died, twenty-six year, come next Sunday."

"You have had a hard time of it, Hannah

—you left with five men children to raise, and the oldest only ten, and the youngest creeping under feet."

"I ain't complaining. The Lord seen me through, and the boys are good boys, if they are scattered."

"I s'pose thirty thousand dollars wouldn't buy your and Alpheus's farms together."

"No, ma'am. And it will be all Alpheus's some day, for the other boys got their sheer, to take out in the world. Alpheus and me, we stuck to the farm. Ellen, I cayn't tell you the way I felt when I handed Al the hundred and fifty-two dollars I had laid by. He was expecting to sell a colt to raise that money; he'd no notion of me having any sich sum. But I was not going to have him sell that colt he wanted to drive; it's Al's besetment he wants to drive a good hoss. That makes me think I better be gitting along with mine; it's not overly warm no more. You see, I cayn't take my time and pleasure, like I used; I got a girl now. Al, he would have me git one."

"What's your hurry? She can look ayfter the supper."

"Hmn!" grunted Mrs. Swift, grimly jocular, "who'll look ayfter the girl? She bust the door off the oven, last time I left her to look ayfter things; had a turkey in and plumb forgot to baste it, and it dried up and bust with a pop like a cannon. Well, pray for patience! maybe, if we both live long enuff, she'll learn something. I tell Al —— " She broke off, startled at her friend's worried look, instead of the smile she had expected. "Air you sick or anything, Ellen?" she asked, in a very gentle tone.

"Oh, I cayn't tell her, any way on earth!" was the thought that had puckered Mrs. Dagget's brows. She did not tell her then; she allowed Mrs. Swift to reproach her for walking recklessly on her lame ankle; she sat passive, while the old woman went into the house to put on the linen duster and large hat that should ward off sun and dust, her conscience pummeling her every second; but, when the gaunt figure reappeared, she took her courage in both hands.

"Hannah," said she, not looking at Mrs.

Swift, "have you heard of Miss Pennell's loss?"

"That girl was visiting at the 'Piscopal minister's? No; was it any nigh kin?"

"No," solemnly, "it wasn't no kin at all; it was her beautiful diamond pin!"

"Is that so?" said Mrs. Swift. She was civilly concerned, but she was not in the least agitated.

Mrs. Dagget looked far more nervous as she continued: "You saw it, didn't you? Wasn't you there when she was packing up to go 'way?"

Yes — indifferently — she had come that day with butter, and she remembered the pin; it was right on the sofy in the front room, with a lot of gewgaws; a kinder pretty pin.

"Pretty?" screamed Mrs. Dagget. "It cost two hundred and twenty dollars! Don't you remember the clothes that girl used to wear? And she gave five dollars to the missionaries! She was dreadful rich!"

"She must 'a' been dreadful keerless, to leave her things round so and lose sich a vallerable pin," said Mrs. Swift, calmly.

"She thinks it was stole. They was called out of the room while she was packing; the girl had a telegraph for Miss Pennell, jest fetched, and she and Mrs. Keith went out together; and when they came back there was the case all right on the sofy with the rest, and she chucked it into her bag; and it was afterward Mrs. Keith wasn't sure something was in, and so they took things out, and the pin was gone. It was jest an empty case."

"Well!"

"When you seen it," the lace slipped out of Mrs. Dagget's shaking fingers, "I don't mean the first time, but when you come back, was anybody in the room?"

"Not a soul," said Mrs. Swift. "I'd got out on the sidewalk, when I missed my little black bag; so I come back, and the door of that front room stood on the jar, and I says, 'Excuse me, ladies,' and went in, got my bag and went out. It was laying right on the sofy, beside that pin." Suddenly Mrs. Swift's eyes glazed, while the words faltered off her tongue. Whether it was the fright on the face of her old friend, or the

blinding flash of recognition in her own
mind, she herself could not have told.
"Why, merciful Lord! I was the last person in that room!" she thought far down
in her soul. "I was in a hurry and I run!
But would anybody dast —— " The blood
was tingling along her old veins; her face
burned red, redder, an intolerable hot scarlet. "Do you mean to say, Ellen Dagget,"
she cried, gripping the other's plump shoulder, "that anybody dast think I come back
for anything 'cept to get my own bag?"

"Mrs. Keith and Miss Pennell, they saw
you," stammered Mrs. Dagget, "and the
hired girl —— "

"Do they think I stole that pin?"

"Oh, lawsey, Hannah, don't look at me
that way. I never thought it — not for a
single minnit! You couldn't!"

"Where did you hear 'bout it?"

Mrs. Dagget, weeping, murmured something about "Simon."

"They been talking 'bout it at the store,"
said Mrs. Swift. Releasing Mrs. Dagget,
she walked uncertainly to the chair where
she had sat in such a different mood. And

Ellen had known about it all the time! She sank down; the village street flooded with sunshine, the small, cheerful houses with their curtains and open windows, the bare-footed children making a joyous din over their ball, Tim Murray's dog chasing the Dilworthy cows westward into a dust spangled gold haze, all the homely peaceful scene wavered and surged before her. But she held herself erect by the arms of her chair; she kept the even pitch of her voice. "Half a dozen times, lately, folks was looking the other way when I passed. Last Sunday, to the song service, when I got up to give my testimony, Brother Given never said a word when I sat down. Yesterday I asked Ann Liza Forest to stop, going by, and get a cup o' tea and some of my green tomato preserve; I never knowed such a thing as her to refuse, but she refused then. That 's what it meant."

"Oh, Hannah dear, I never believed a word!"

"I been a member since I was called, at the age of fifteen. I ain't fallen from grace, as I know. I ain't had no great to give, but I gave willing of what I had. Alpheus worked six days to help build the church, and we lent the teams to haul lumber. I always paid my debts prompt, though me and my children went without shoes more 'n one time to do it. I sold the red heifer to Brother Given for twenty dollars, because he had my word, though Squire Dilworthy offered me twenty-six. Simon Dagget knows my apples and my berries run jest the same to the bottom of the box."

"It is only because they saw you, and you going to Davenport and coming back last week, and having money to give Alpheus, and his not selling the colt — but nobody thinks it — not really — but I knew you could make it — explain it — and oh, Hannah, you didn't think I, long 's we 've known each other, and the way you was to me when little Eddy died, I couldn't — I —— " Here poor Mrs. Dagget, at her wits' end, hobbled across to the other chair and wept over the linen duster.

"Ellen Dagget, you shet up! Crying right on the front porch, before the whole

town! I ain't going to let this down me.
Get up and set down decent."

In such Spartan semblance did Hannah
Swift retreat, notwithstanding the world
reeled about her. She would not take a sip
of an assassinating liquor that slandered
the name of brandy, kept "for sickness"
by Mrs. Dagget, and regarded with awe by
the household — as well it might be! She
would not have Rufe, the boy of all work,
fetch her horses from the store. She remained about twenty minutes longer, mi-
nutely and pertinaciously questioning Mrs.
Dagget; and then she went to the store herself, and drove by the piazza with her elbows
at a sharp angle, erect and defiant to the
last glimpse.

"Lord knows whether I done right to tell
her," moaned poor Mrs. Dagget — who com-
pared her own sensations, telling Simon of
it, to a rag just free from the wringer—"but
it did seem she had ought to know! And
now I must find that chicken pie to send over
to Marcia Wright."

At that moment, Marcia was lifting her
heavy veil, as if by the action she could lift

the heavier visions that encompassed her, and shaking off the dust that her distempered fancy feigned a symbol of the soil cast on her nature by a hideous experience.

Eight months ago, the two forlorn explorers into the world had crept back, like wounded animals, to their old home. Mrs. Wright, stricken with a mortal disease, had a homesick longing to die among the familiar scenes near her husband's grave. Marcia could not oppose her. She had no hopes, and but one fear, and that drew closer, every day of a failing life.

To return to Flowering Bridge meant merely a little heavier weight on her heart, a wrench or two more of the rack for her conscience.

Then she met Alpheus Swift again.

He had few of the graces that she used to worship, but which now seemed to her the charms of the snake. Al was a man that other men respected. He was strong, he was gentle, he had the delicacy of a good heart; and he was infinitely kind and thoughtful to her mother. Insensibly, the sense of his worthiness, that she had kept through all the disenchantment of her wretched married life, was transmuted into a keener feeling.   But this only revealed to her a new sensibility to pain in her numbed heart, since there were reasons that her conscience could not evade, why she might not yield to his tenderness.   To be sure, one of these reasons had been removed of late; but there was always the other.   Indeed, so worn and shamed was she that she almost esteemed it a fresh sin of hers that she should dare to love at all.

Even Mrs. Swift would have pitied her to-day, could she have read the thoughts of the woman she hated.

The carriage had passed the last straggling houses of the village; Marcia saw tree-tops over the horses' heads, maple-tops waving greenly, safe from the dust of the traveled roads.   The omnibus and the hearse were already through the gate. There was a white arch above it, and black letters painted on the arch.   She could see the graves and the white stones.   She felt the carriage settle backward in its place; the driver — she had known him from a boy — was at the door, his reins over his arm. "Say, let me help you out," he said, "the hosses will stand." But she thanked him and walked to the grave alone, before Mrs. Pratt could scramble out of the last buggy. The sun dazed her, and she stumbled on her black skirts. By the side of the road was the open grave, lined with fir boughs. It was kind, she thought, in the sexton, to take away thus the raw horror of the upturned earth; and then immediately she knew it was not the sexton that she should thank. Mrs. Pratt came and stood by her side; the slender young man in the surplice opened his prayer book. Dully, Marcia felt grateful for the companionship, grateful that it was not Brother Given, whom her mother had not trusted, reciting those sentences of immeasurable faith and hope. But it was more and more dully because her head ached so queerly and it took all her will to stand. There were moments when she forgot where she was and had the old sensation of needing to hurry in order to get home to her mother. She would be roused by a pang like a knife stab, and see and hear, but directly she would be away again. In one of these conscious moments, she was aware of the perfume of lilies. A young man, standing at her side, held a great bunch of them; and while she was struggling to focus her brain on them enough to recognize them and their connection with her, this man stepped forward and laid them on the coffin-lid. There were other flowers; but these were exotics from the city, to which the streamers of white satin ribbons lent a formal pomp. Once, during her sickness, her mother had said that she liked flowers tied with white ribbon — she should like some on her coffin; because of that speech, Marcia had tied the roses from Mrs. Dagget with ribbon. She perceived that another had remembered also. Remembered what? She was drifting again. There was a creaking of straps, a slight bustle among the men. Why, it was her mother's coffin that they lowered — her mother's! and she must go back to that empty home! She swayed to one side; she did not care any longer that she was going to faint, the anguish of her loss possessed her; she did not even know that Alpheus and Mrs. Pratt led her to the carriage. Alpheus got in after her; but he had said to Mrs. Pratt: "Won't you go home with her?" And she had answered: "No, I won't, Alpheus Swift. Nobody can comfort that poor girl like you; you git right in and do it."

Therefore, when Marcia revived, she saw him fanning her.

Six years had made a man out of the shy and awkward lad that she knew. He was neither shy nor awkward, having the manner of a man used to consideration from others. He was dressed neatly and tastefully, though hardly in the fashion of the city. His fair, composed features were like his mother's, but they were suffused with a deep tenderness.

"I don't think she would have minded, dear," were his first words, "and I couldn't bear to have you go back alone."

As she did not reply, "I have two things to tell you," said he, "for I don't know when you will let me see you again. I saw your mother that last day you went out with the work, and I told her."

Marcia's breath came more quickly.

"She was very kind. She said she would be glad to have you marry me; she said it made her happy."

Then Marcia recalled the delirium of those subsequent days, comprehending with a weakening of the heart the reason for that illusion of her marriage.

"You did make her happy," she cried; "she was happy at the end." The tears swept her words away. They would not come to soften her own anguish, but at the thought of the peace that he had brought her mother, they rained down her cheeks. She wept for a long time, while he sat beside her, not so much as venturing to touch her hand, lest he should divert her grief into the channel of a crueler pain. Only, he laid a fresh handkerchief from his own pocket very softly on her knee. She used it mechanically, then she looked at him and said: "I don't believe there ever was a man treated as badly as you that could forgive so!"

"Oh, there's lots," said he, "you were fair to me, Marcia — but never mind the past ; you are here, and I am here, and you shall make it up to me if you want to. This doesn't seem the place for this kind of talk; but if your mother sees us, she understands. I am sure she would have me take every chance. Marcia, I have just come back from Anamosa this morning. What I told your mother is all correct, like in the warden's letter. He died a month ago."

"I didn't doubt it before; but you were kind to go, Al."

"I promised her. They told me he died penitent," said Al, doggedly, "and he hoped you'd forgive him."

"I do forgive him; it wasn't all his fault, Al — I wasn't so patient as I ought to have been."

Al said nothing ; his mouth bore a peculiar resemblance to his mother's. He recalled with a bracing sensation his one personal encounter with Marcia's late husband and the severe thrashing he (Alpheus) had given him.

"Was he comfortable in the hospital?" said Marcia.

"Yes."

"I mean, did he have the little things he wanted — fruit and wine and such things?"

"Yes."

She threw back her veil and showed him the ghost of a smile. "Al, I could always see through you. I believe you sent him those things yourself!"

"Yes, I did," said Al, frowning. "I supposed you would fret, someway, if he didn't get them. Him — I didn't care a rap about *him!* I didn't believe in his palaver."

A pause, during which Al coughed a harassing lump down his throat, but it left his tones husky as he asked: "Is there any other reason you got for not marrying me, Marcia?"

"You know it, Al."

"You mean mother? Well, Marcia, you know what I think. I love my mother, and I'm willing to make any sacrifice in reason for her. She can have her house and the biggest of the farms, and I'll let her have

her say about the stock.   I know what I owe
to her ——.''

"Maybe what you don't know is how she
loves you."

His answer was not the answer that she
expected, although one natural enough in a
lover.   What he said was: "You are an
angel!"

But he didn't think it natural that she
should begin to cry.   "Al," she implored
him, "I disobeyed my mother, and look
what misery and shame it brought on us
both — on the innocent as well as the
guilty!   Oh, Al, don't you go and want to
do the same thing!   Do you think now I'm
just beginning to realize what it is to lose a
mother, I could be plotting to break your
mother's heart?   She couldn't bear it to
have you marry me!   She despises me.
Oh, she has got the right to despise me —
hush, dear," at a passionate gesture from
the young man — "I know you don't, but
she doesn't know anything about me except
my silly, wicked folly!   It would be wicked
to bring such sorrow to her, Al!   God would
punish us — oh, I wouldn't mind His pun-

ishing me, a poor, broken thing as I am, but you — you — my darling ——"

Never before had she used a caressing word like that to him, and she could see the blood surge up his forehead, and his eyes flash. She moved away from him. "Don't be afraid, dear," he said, gently; "I'm not going to kiss you! I want to, and there's no moral harm in it; but I won't, not if you don't want me to. See, dear, just this!" and, turning back the hem of her black glove, he kissed her wrist, not ardently, but with a solemn and reverent tenderness. "I won't worry you any more now; I can wait," said he, "I know you belong to me."

"Yes," said she. They only spoke of trivial things after this, until they reached the house. At the gate he helped her out, and Mrs. Dagget herself opened the door and took Marcia in her arms.

II.

Shaken though she was, Hannah Swift did not lose her reasoning powers; but the more she rummaged the details of the evidence, the uglier it looked! They must have searched the house thoroughly; if they

had not, and the pesky thing — which, to
Hannah's mind, it was a sin and a shame
for any Christian woman to be wearing anyhow — had been overlooked, most like it had
been swept up, carted off, flung into the
ravine that the Dyers and the Pratts used
too, and Lord help anybody to find anything
in that mux!

And there were the three women to prove
that she was the last creature in the house
before the diamond disappeared. Not so
much as a bird or a dog or a cat to lay the
blame on! The Keiths kept none of them.
She could not even prove that she had the
money given to Al, for it was the piecemeal
accumulation of years, and unhappily she
had not put it in the bank. Now this sudden
wealth bore witness against her.

Only one plan promised anything —
namely, to write to Davenport in order that
she might get proof that she had not gone
to a jeweler's or sold any diamond.

But this was a gigantic undertaking for
an unready writer. She must needs employ
a penman; and whom? She recoiled with
an inexpressible fright from the thought

of applying to Alpheus. That her son
might hear of the charge was her daily terror. She watched him like a cat. His fits
of abstraction, his ominous indifference to
what he ate, scared her. She tried to think
that he was "only fussing 'bout Marshy."
Yet not a week ago Marcia had been the
specter!

Sunday came, and Hannah went to church
as usual, staying over to the evening service.

She noted every averted glance, every
chilled greeting; very likely she suspected
chill and aversion where they did not exist.

At the evening service Brother Given
spoke on secret sins. He was a handsome,
portly man, whose loud voice and imposing
stature gave an appearance of more decision
than he will claim at the judgment day. He
talked with a certain rude eloquence, telling pathetic tales in illustration of his theme.
Many of the women wiped their eyes, but
some merely used their handkerchiefs as a
screen behind which they could look safely
at the Swift pew. Hannah did not flinch in
a muscle; she breathed slowly and regularly

and she suffered as only a proud woman can.

"Confession and restitootion," roars Brother Given, "oh, my sinful brother — oh, my sinful sister—they alone can cleanse the soul! But make no mistake" — leaning over the pulpit cushions and smiting the palm of one hand with the fingers of the other, while his voice sinks to a confidential semitone — "restitootion, restitootion is the greatest duty! Confession, I say boldly, is not as important as restitootion. Why, suppose, let us say, that you have lost property — stock, or money, or land, or jewelry — any sort of property; do you want your poor sinful brother, who took it, to come back and confess, as much as you want your property back? You say, 'No, of course not, Brother Given!' I can imagine a case where the wronged one would say: "I don't ask you to confess; you have led a respectable life, you may have an innercent family to consider. Make restitootion — give it back, and go in peace!' Go and sin no more; that's the main point. Will Sister Pratt please lead us in prayer?"

Not a few of the listeners felt that Sister Pratt neglected an opportunity of grace; for, while she dutifully prayed that we might be given strength to repent and cleanse ourselves from undiscovered sin, she also prayed that we be preserved from prying into other folks' sins, and from uncharitable and suspicious minds.

Mrs. Swift waited to shake hands with Sister Pratt at the door.   She did not thank her for her prayer, but she told her that she hoped she (Sister Pratt) would come and see her new crazy-quilt.   "I got a hull lot of pieces left over," said Mrs. Swift; "maybe some on 'em would do for yours.   You 're real welcome to them !"

She was speaking when the preacher appeared and would have edged by the group; instantly she stopped him.

"Brother Given," said she, in a clear voice of good compass, "you give us a powerful discourse, and all true; but what of folks that air suspicioned and cayn't confess nor restitoot neither, 'cause they ain't done it?"

"Surely, sister, such cases will be cleared. I was only alluding to certain guilt."

"Well, now, 'tain't so easy to be certain." Thus good Mrs. Pratt put in her word, as she placed her sturdy figure in the small remaining portion of the passage-way. "I'd a lesson 'bout that, this very weēk; didn't I bile my currant jel 'most 'way to nothing, jest 'cause I was so fool certain I'd put the sugar in! I'd a-measured it and set it away in the pantry, and I knowed I'd put it in; and why in mercy didn't that jel thick up? But I *hadn't* put it in, all the same! It is a sight easier making mistakes than taking pains!"

Meekly Brother Given agreed, and clutchèd a passing brother, under whose convoy he made his retreat. He was a peace loving man, who had dealt with the scandal according to the lights of others rather than his own; and he was by no means assured in his soul.

Monday and Tuesday, Mrs. Swift did her duty by the family washing. Wednesday, she had occasion to come to town. Her road led past an unsavory restaurant and secret liquor den of the type that curses rural districts. Half a dozen youths lolled on the bench outside the fly-specked window, trying to persuade themselves that they were bad young men. They smoked and spat vociferously. At the moment of Mrs. Swift's passing, the wag of the party made a joke, and there was a burst of coarse laughter. She was sure that they were laughing at her, and whipped up her horses, her old face aflame. She did not rein the horses in for a long way; indeed, her reckless driving had nearly caused her to run over Marcia Wright on a crossing. Marcia carried a great bundle. She looked white and tired, in her black clothes.

Mrs. Swift's elbows widened to shorten her reins, then she lashed her horses' backs with them and frowned; she had resisted an extraordinary impulse to bid Marcia get into her wagon. "It's right on my way to take her home," she had thought; then with a sneer at her own movement of compassion, "the two outcasts together — that would be a show!"

"I s'pose she does have a hard time,"

she answered an invisible opponent half a
score of times, on the way home, "but she
deserves it; I don't!"

Whereupon the opponent retorted: "How
do you know? Do you know, or have you
been jealous and ready to hate her because
your boy loved her?" And the opponent
asked questions about Marcia's sufferings,
and stung Hannah's torpid imagination into
picturing a disgrace like her own.

Such thoughts gave her bad nights. She
grew haggard. Alpheus urged her to con-
sult a doctor. She knew that he watched
her; and she, in turn, watched him with an
agony of suspicion. The next time she
drove to town, she went with a purpose.
"Might's well ask her as anybody," said
Hannah Swift; "I kin pay her."

Therefore, when she saw Marcia on the
street, she overwhelmed the young woman
with amazement by asking her to ride. She
had leisure, sitting on the same seat with
Marcia, to study the peaked oval of her
face, the hollow cheeks that she remembered so blooming, the sunken eyes and the

careworn lines about the mouth that used to wear so insolent a smile.

"Yes," she said to herself, "she does look distressid; I guess she has had it hot and heavy, and maybe she didn't deserve all on 't!"

Aloud she said: "Marshy Wright, I guess you know what folks say 'bout me."

"Yes, ma'am," quavered Marcia.

"Well, do you believe it 's true?"

"No, ma'am; of course not."

"Course not? What do you know about it, you 're so certain?"

"I know *you!*" said Marcia, with her glimmer of a smile. Nothing dies so hard as the sense of humor, and Marcia's sometimes showed vitality, still.

"Hmn," said Mrs. Swift, "you 're the fust to take 'count of that. Well, how be I to prove the lies ain't true, Marshy Wright?"

Marcia colored, but she answered firmly: "I am sure it was not stolen at all; I am going to sew at Mrs. Keith's next week, and maybe I can see better then how it could be lost. Then you—you could show you didn't pawn any diamond when you went to Davenport."

"That's so, Marshy; but I got to have somebody write for me." And she stopped, hardly knowing how to ask Marcia.

"If—if I could do it, Mrs. Swift?" said Marcia.

"I guess you could do it if you wanted to," said Mrs. Swift.

One bit of information gleaned from the subsequent conversation consoled her; she gathered that Alpheus knew nothing of the evil gossip—at least, he had not discussed it with Marcia; and by the fierce leap of her pulses at Marcia's assurance, the poor mother knew what had been that dread. Really, Al did know nothing; the people of Flowering Bridge were a kindly sort, and would have been shocked at the idea of taking a son into confidence about the dishonor of his mother.

But you may be sure Marcia told him how civilly Mrs. Swift had greeted her. Al spoke no word of gratitude; but he bought his mother a new gown, and praised all the poor maid's disasters in bread, rashly imputing them to her mistress.

All this while, the small community was in a state of agitation out of all experience. It seemed terrible to suspect a woman of stainless probity, a mother in Israel who had kept her word to her hurt; and yet— who else took the diamonds? They were there when she left the house for the first time, they were left there by the others, they were gone after her second secret visit; and suddenly she has a large unsuspected sum of money, just when it is needed. Mrs. Dagget's explanation of the return for the black bag might be granted without affecting the case against Mrs. Swift. Suppose she did go back merely to get the bag; she found herself alone with temptation sudden and great, she did not see the three women watching her behind the lattice, she thought herself safe, and she had snatched the diamond and fled.

On the whole, public opinion drifted further and further away from any theory of innocence.

Again Sunday came. Mrs. Swift sat in

her pew, erect and calm as iron.   Brother Given shrank from her steady eyes.   If she could only have guessed how afraid he was, and how safe she was from any sinister implications from him!

During the week, the replies to her letters began to come.   By the end of the week, all Marcia's correspondents had answered her inquiries.   The letters accounted for every minute of Mrs. Swift's time in the city; Marcia had done her task well.

As Mrs. Swift read them, she smiled. Now, Marcia could not remember a smile on the grim woman's face; it was wonderful how the novel radiance altered those harsh features.

"You done well, Marshy," she muttered; "you're a good girl!"   And she told Mrs. Dagget that Marcia Wright was not "nigh sich a fool's she looked."   From any one else, this might seem a mitigated compliment; but it approached enthusiasm on the part of Mrs. Swift, and was so received by her friend, who, she assured Simon, felt as if the world were coming to an end, and was obliged to "stay herself" with a punch.

Punch in that temperate household meant a teaspoonful of brandy to a large tumblerful of water; and, notwithstanding the baleful nature of the brandy—bought at a drug store under oath that it was for medicinal purposes only—had never harmed a mortal. Hannah Swift declined the punch, saying that she feared it might go to her head, and she wanted all her wits about her, because she was going to "dress up" and visit Mrs. Keith.

It was part of the curious reticence used in the whole affair, that the two women should have had no direct dealings regarding it.

"Now I am going to have it out with her!" said Hannah.

Home she went, with a lighter heart in her breast than she had carried for weeks, and straightway laid out her best black bombazine gown, her bonnet, and, as a portion of her garb of state, her fine black cachemire shawl.

"Sun's hot, but I don't need to put it on till I git right up to the house," she considered; "I never could feel dressed up in jest my body and no cape or nothing. For the land's sake! if I ain't tore out a hunk of the fringe! It's gitting in and out of that pesky top-buggy, that's what done it. And I got to have that buggy to-day, too. I told Mike to wash it off every time I used it, but I'll bet anything he ain't; and goodness knows when I used it last!"

On the spur of the thought, she hurried out to the barn, knowing that Mike was disposed to neglect the "top-buggy," which, indeed, was used rarely. Sure enough, there it stood with the mud caked on its tires.

"Well, Mike and me has got to have a reckoning, right straight," said Hannah.

But fate had willed to spare the erring Mike. Mrs. Swift, who was slapping the cushions into place, all at once dived her gray head under the seat, uttered a shrill quavering cry, and sank in a heap on the floor.

Between her limp fingers, the great diamond of Miss Pennell's lost brooch winked at her like an evil eye! A few strands of black worsted clung to the gold setting.

"The fringe of my shawl!" groaned Hannah Swift. "I must 'a' switched it off the sofy, and it caught; and when the fringe tore out, gitting outer the buggy, it fell off, and it's lay there all this time, for I ain't had the buggy out sence. Oh, Lordamassy, 'twas *me* stole it, ayfter all!"

I hesitate to describe the blackness of the next hours for that honest, haughty old soul. No confession could set her right with her world now; there would always be a question whether she had not invented the story, being frightened at the consequences of her crime.

Somehow she did get herself and the diamonds back to the house, back to her own chamber. The instincts of a pious life made her sink on her knees by the bed, just as she had sunk there in the other great crisis of her life, when her husband died.

"Oh, Elder, if you was only here to tell it to!" the crushed heart wailed. She tried to pray, but her first words were stopped on her lips by a searing flash of thought: "Is it a judgment, O Lord?" she sobbed, wildly, "'cause I held myself so high and didn't show mercy to sinners! Now, ain't I be going to be 'lowed to hold myself innercent? Oh, Lord, have I got to own them fools was right?"

In the whole world, who would believe her now? Yes, there was one — a woman who had known an equal bitterness, a woman whom she had defamed and despised and misjudged. "Marshy 'd know how I felt, and she 'd believe me, too," she thought; "but I got to give it all up, if I go now. I cayn't do that — I cayn't, Lord, I cayn't!"

Nevertheless, two hours later, she knocked at Marcia Wright's door. She marched into her errand without preliminaries:

"Marshy, I don't know what you 'll say, but I jest found out I stole that pin!"

"Then you took it by mistake," said Marcia; "how did it happen?"

Before the end of Mrs. Swift's narrative, her cheeks were flushed and her eyes shining; she looked like her old self.

"And now," Mrs. Swift concluded, dismally, "I don't see nothing for it but to take up my cross and go over to Mrs. Keith's with the pin and tell her the hull story. Maybe they'll make me confess in church, too, and folks won't believe me nohow; but if they don't, the Lord knows I done my best."

"I wouldn't do any such thing," said Marcia, firmly; "don't you remember what Brother Given said about restitution being better than confession? I guess he ought to know. All you are bound to do is to get that diamond back to Mrs. Keith; and that's all Mrs. Keith wants, either!"

"But what will I say to the woman?"

Marcia rose, a new energy in every poise of her slim young figure; she laid her hands on Hannah's bowed shoulders, she fixed her shining eyes full on Hannah's despairing face, her voice was sweet and high. "Mrs. Swift," said she, "can you trust me to give that pin back?"

"Marshy," Hannah Swift answered, solemnly, "I kin trust you with anything in this world."

And then a most strange thing happened: Marcia, with that transfigured face, bent nearer and kissed her. So strange a thing was it that in all her bewildered misery she kept returning to it and to her own sensations.

"It was awful funny; and what was funnier, I kinder liked it!" said she.

That which might have occurred to her as yet a stranger circumstance than the caress or her own feelings was the further fact that, in spite of knowing no more than her horses regarding Marcia's plans, she had unhesitatingly promised secrecy.

She went home with a timid, unwarranted, unaccountable hope in her company. But the night was long, and Mrs. Dagget, who appeared about noon, exclaimed at her pallor.

"Never mind; I got news to raise the dead," thought the kind woman; "but I got to break it gentle."

By way of breaking it gently, she fell on Mrs. Swift's neck and burst into tears.

"Ellen Dagget, what is the matter with you?" cried Hannah, sternly. "If you got bad news, tell it; don't go to scaring me this way!"

"Oh, it ain't bad news; it's good. They've found Miss Pennell's pin!"

Mrs. Swift's knees gave way under her; she dropped into the nearest chair.

"Found?" she gasped, feebly.

"Yes, found. You come right into the other room, where the girl won't be running in on us, and set down, and I'll tell you the whole from beginning to end. You poor thing?" Thus mingling sympathy and command, Mrs. Dagget propelled her friend into the shelter of the dim "best room," and the nearest rocking chair.

"Now, this is the way of it," said she: "Marcia Wright, she's been sewing for Mrs. Keith, and she is working on a plum-colored dress that has got those big, expensive buttons on it to match; and some-way, this morning, first thing, one of the buttons got lost. Well, Marcia set 'em all to hunting, and hunted herself, but no button! Finally, says Marcia: 'Could it have got into the rags, and where did they keep them?' Well, they kept the good big rags in the rag-bag, and the little scraps and scrids they jest chucked in the stove. Marcia said they might's well look in both—button wouldn't burn up, if rags did. And first they looked in the rag-bag, and then they overhauled that stove, and carted every last dud out of it; and whilst they were looking, the hired girl gave a screech, and Mrs. Keith looks in—she mistrusted it was a mouse, and you know she ain't 'fraid of nothing—and she pulled it out—Miss Pennell's diamond pin!"

"Oh, Lord have mercy!" said Mrs. Swift.

"Yes, there 'twas, good 's ever, jest smouched a little. Mrs. Keith says it all come to her in a flash. That was the room they was packing in, you know. There was a lot of papers and stuff on the floor, and, soon 's she put the things in the bag, she told the girl to clear up; and she put the papers in the stove, and that pin must have been in them."

"Hadn't they looked in the stove?"

"Why, yes, I guess they had; but it was kinder slipped down in a corner, and I guess they didn't poke round much. You see, Miss Pennell was so swearing certain

she put the pin in the case. It 's jest another case like Sister Pratt's jel! You
cayn't be sure of nothing 'cept original sin,
I say. Mrs. Keith, she feels real upset
about you and how folks have misjudged
you. She was for hiring a livery and coming right out to see you. She didn't seem
to think of the expense at all. But Marcia
— Marcia 's got real good sense, Hannah!"

"I know it," said Hannah, meekly.

"Marcia, she says: 'I wouldn't, Mrs.
Keith; I wouldn't never name it to her,
since you never have. I 'd go and talk to
Mrs. Dagget,' says Marcia. And that 's
jest what she did; and I made the boy
hitch right up, and told Lucy Dagget to
give her pa what she could git for dinner,
and I come here fast 's I could. Mrs. Keith
wants you to know how she feels. She
does feel real bad — why, she couldn't have
got a livery for less 'n two dollars, and she
would have come right off if Marcia hadn't
stopped her. She says she don't blame you
much if you cayn't forgive her —— "

"But I do — I do from my heart," cried
Hannah; "and I thank Marcia and you.

And oh, Ellen, if I didn't need never to hear a word more about it again!"

"Bless your poor heart, you never shall!" said Mrs. Dagget, wiping her eyes.

Flowering Bridge agrees that Mrs. Swift's conduct in burying malice is admirable. Everybody felt a little ashamed at the outcome of the scandal, and everybody was inclined to under-estimate his own distrust. Of course, Sister Swift would not at her age begin to purloin diamond pins! No one had really supposed such a thing. But Al certainly was puzzled at the sudden flood of compliments that he received for his mother — whose gifts and good qualities, from her eyesight to her generosity, had honorable mention — and at the extent of neighborly good-will taking the form of preserves. However, he was too happy and too grateful to his mother, at this time, to find any appreciation of her extravagant.

Hannah herself had mighty wrestlings of conscience.

"Marshy, air you sure there wan't no lies told?" was her first question when the two met again.

"Not a lie," replied Marcia, cheerfully.

"But, Marshy, you had to say something, the time they found it; what did you say, Marshy?"

"Oh, I said: 'Gracious goodness!'"

Possibly Marcia's conscience is rather Western than the undiluted inheritance of the Puritans, for it has given her no twinges; only, sometime, she hopes Mother Swift will consent to her telling Al.

Mrs. Swift walks less firmly now, over her neighbors' faults; she is less caustic in her speech, and slower to wrath, than of yore; she has even asked the pastor's family to tea.

"Tribberlation," says Brother Given, "has brought forth grace!"

The Dilemma
of Sir Guy the Neuter

The Dilemma
of Sir Guy the Neuter.*

❦

I had not loved thee, dear, so much,
Loved I not honor more.—*Richard Lovelace.*

THERE are two portraits remaining of
Sir Guy Paget, later Baron Ellesmere.
One of them hangs in the old hall to which
his descendants have spared its Elizabethan
state. No one can name the painter; probably he was one of the Dutch artists who
were attracted to England by Holbein's
success.

The paint has cracked in minute and
irregular diamonds all over the canvas; and
behind this network of the old spider, Time,
you see Sir Guy's face and his supple and
elegant figure, down past the half of his
comely legs. He is in court dress, as he

---

*The bishop in this story was a most real and manful
man, to whose memory I offer this slight tribute. His story
may be found in any history of England.

77

was wont to appear before her majesty, Mary I of England: cloth of silver and white taffeta, jewels sparkling from his sword hilt, and a "marten chain" wound about his square white velvet cap.

I judge that, at this time, he may have owned twenty-eight or nine years. He has the dark hair of the Pagets (fine and straight, I discover elsewhere) brushed upward in the fashion of the day. His slight beard hardly disguises the beautiful oval of his face. His tawny gray eyes, though not large, are full of fire. The nose is the rather long, well formed nose of Holbein's portraits; the chin is firm; and the delicate lips are relaxed by a fine, half-melancholy, half-satiric smile.

The other portrait, a miniature by Hilliard, taken in Elizabeth's reign, shows the same graceful beauty, not effeminate, yet certainly not robust, and the same smile, which I am quite unable to describe. In the miniature, Lord Ellesmere wears armor, being thus represented at the instance of his wife, whom he tenderly loved and who was proud of his martial exploits. He was, indeed, a valiant and fortunate commander; but it was at the court, not in the field, that he mended the estate of a poor gentleman into that of a great lord; and it is the courtier who smiles that haunting and elusive smile.

Perhaps I am reading my own meanings into this dead courtier's face, or taking them, modernized in spite of myself, from the manuscript story which he left to his grandson. He left other records of strange passages in his life, some of them concerning very great personages, indeed; possibly it is for that reason they have been destroyed. Tradition also accuses him of "diuers Sonets the wich were extream commended of Master Philip Sidney." But they have gone their way to oblivion, all the same. I know of no line of Guy Paget's extant outside these musty old pages, the narrative of a tragic and bewildering episode.

Next to his celebrated uncle, the man who most influenced Guy's life was an almost forgotten hero, Robert Ferrars,

Bishop of St. Davids. His first meeting with Ferrars was in this wise:

During the autumn of 1549, Edward VI, then being on the throne, and the Catholic rebellion just happily suppressed, Master Paget rode through Devonshire with dispatches from his uncle to the Bishop of St. Davids. The bishop and his wife had gone to Devonshire to visit Sir Peter Carew, the bishop's brother-in-law, and afterward convoy his daughter, Lady Godsalve, with them to Wales, because of the prospective absence of her father and husband in Italy on a diplomatic mission. Guy was to meet the bishop in a little Devonshire village. The sun was passing into the west as he came in sight of the village. He rode unattended, for his business was private. "Though of young years," says another chronicler, "Master Paget was greatly esteemed and trusted by his uncle, and much employed by him in secret affairs of state."

The mire of the foul ways had splashed Guy's riding boots, as well as the cloak of fine Flemish cloth which he wore to pro-

tect his doublet of "wanchett blue velvet
guarded with silver." Yet for all the travel
stains, he must have looked a gallant and
handsome young gentleman. Not a very
light hearted one at this moment, however,
though he expected, presently, to see his
sweetheart. He gazed about him with a
bitter smile. The sunshine bathed the
moist green meadows where the sheep were
grazing. Kingcups and cuckoo blossoms
and all the dazzling ranks of the autumn
flowers were freshly sprung along the road-
side or waving above the hedgerows; and
sloes showed their sleek black sides on the
blackthorn bushes. A little brook flashed
across the open before it dipped into the
shade of wooded banks. You could see,
from Guy's point of vision, orchards and
groves, and single majestic oaks or horse-
chestnuts dappling the plain with rich shadow; and harvests waving their dull gold;
and hills to break the soft curves of the
landscape on the horizon line. Directly before him the highway slipped out of sight
among the steep roofs of the village.

The scene was one of just such gentle

and pensive loveliness as English poets, in
all ages, have delighted to praise, but now
it was a loveliness disheveled and woeful.
The ruined harvests were tumbled over
their fields. Ragged gaps had been slashed
in the hedges; deep furrows were plowed
in the greensward; how, was easy to know
from the broken cannon wheels, the bleach-
ing bones of horses, rusted pieces of weap-
ons and armor, and all the hideous litter of
warfare still cumbering the ground. A long,
transverse ridge of raw earth marked the
common grave of king's men and rebels. In
like wise the black heaps of ashes and
charred timbers, here and there, meant
that the soldiers had burned the cottages.
So near Guy that his horse's nostrils di-
lated with the smoke, a few rafters were
still smoldering. They had taken the wayside cross out of its socket, hacked it into
the semblance of a gallows, and swung from
it a man in a tattered frieze frock. His
clouted soles were barely a foot from the
embers.

Guy frowned and rode away. The main
street of the village was blocked halfway

by an ancient Norman church. Here, again, Guy saw signs of that furious time. The lead was peeled from the roof, and the tower stripped of its bells. Zealots had smashed the noble windows, leaving only jagged points like red and blue flames to cling to the cusps and mullions. Within, the choir, bare of all that the piety of ages had bestowed, altars, ornaments, crucifixes, images, held only an oaken communion table; and the walls had been "white limned" so roughly that the floor and even the table were bespattered. Through the trefoil above the group of lancet windows on the north side of the tower, fronting the street, a great beam was run, from which dangled a rope, its purpose plainly indicated by the loop and swinging end.

A crowd of half-grown lads craned their necks at the noose; and a half-score men-at-arms made "scurril jests."

Guy kept his way on down the street. It was a narrow street, unpaved, drained by open gutters. The houses abutted on it directly. Most of them were of timber and plaster, two stories high, divided by a projecting string-course. The booths of the tradesmen were below, their dwellings were above. Evidently the town was astir in some unwonted fashion, for heads crowded the windows and doorways, and little groups of citizens, with troubled faces, talked together at the street corners. Guy easily distinguished the inn by its sign of the gilded swan. It was a timber house of some architectural pretensions, built about a quadrangle. The façade had the lawless picturesqueness of the epoch, with its Gothic gables, its large, deeply recessed windows, shapen with the Tudor arch, and divided into many lights, its carven dripstones and cornices, and its porch and porch chamber supported on Ionic pillars. The porch seats were filled with the village magnates, and the tapster in his leather apron and crumpled white hose was serving them to great stoups of beer.

No landlord was to be seen (Guy learned afterward that he was a timorous man who shunned the wagging of tongues), but his wife displayed a new violet kirtle and her black eyes and red cheeks in the doorway.

She, alone, was unabashed by Guy's approach; she greeted him courteously, and having rendered his horse to the hostler and bade the tapster fetch a fresh tankard, she continued her speech. "Marry," she cried, "though they do hang him, I say he was a kind man; many a dirge and placebo hath he said for a poor body, nor axed for the dirge groat. And which o' the new priests would ha' tarried like him i' the plague time?"

"He feared naught"—it was a red-faced yeoman who took up the word. "Lord, how stout he did crack at the usurers and sheep mongers, and the forestallers and regrators!"

There was a cautious acquiescence in nods, with side glances at Guy.

A young man would have told of the equally notable drubbing administered to these hated personages by Master Latimer, the king's preacher; but it was clear that young Dobson was suspected of making his travels too conspicuous; they, his elders and betters, were never in London; his own father checked him:

"Aye, aye, lad, 'twas famous fine, no doubt, but good Sir Giles was broad spoken enow for me."

"By likelihood, he was too broad spoken," said a burgher, "'tis claimed he practiced with the headiness of the multitude; and sure he said the mass the old way."

"Well, they ha' swept us good clean of the mass, now," the tapster rejoined, grimly, "and ta'en the roods down, too. Poor Hobb be hanging to one now."

The citizens exchanged black looks.

"They will sweep the land good clean of religion," cried an old man in a threadbare sarcenet gown. "The nobles be jeerers and mockers, riotous and bloody and evil livers, the young men be neuters, of no faith. They fear neither God nor the devil. The merchants have the Gospel swimming on their lips; but, Lord, how they oppress the poor! They keep their wool and their cloth till it be beyond a poor man's buying; and it weareth no time, for the naughtiness of the making. Rich men will show no compassion to the poor. I say there was never a time when the rich were so cruel to the poor. All kinds of bestial be so high a poor man cannot live. When I was a young man, eggs were a penny a dozen, and 'twas a penny a pound for beef or mutton or veal, and white meat a penny farthing, and neck or legs two farthings. But now the new lords and the clerking knights have enclosed the commons so a poor man cannot keep a cow or pig for the comfort of it."

"Yea, and how the rents be raised!" said the yeoman.

"Wot ye, good people," said a portly mercer, "how this our native country be sore decayed, so 'tis to be feared we may fall a prey to our enemies for lack of men? Everywhere be the people sore minished. Where, in a few years agone, were ten or twelve hundred, be scarce four hundred now, and where did use to be fifty plows and good houses of husbandry, now will be but a shepherd and his dog. And the husbandmen be so pined and famished they be fain to eat acorns, they say."

"Yea," young Dobson interrupted, eagerly, "'sheep and cattle that be ordained to be eaten of men have devoured the men,'

quoth Master Latimer; and worthy Master
Beçon in his book, the 'Jewel of Joy'——" ·

But the crowd would have nothing of
young Dobson or his new lights. The landlady sent a bell-like Devonshire voice above
the din of criticism. "Nay, go to, lad, I perceive, as the saying is, a blind man doth
swallow many a fly. The new priests talk
of charity, but it's from the teeth forward.
Yea, we have a hot gospeler here, that got
our monk's chantry lands. Ye wot well how
that the monks were good landlords. But
this new lord hath enclosed the commons
and so raised his rents and pulled and polled
his tenants that a meanie of them have lost
their farms and must beg on the roads or
fall to picking and stealing. There was one
poor simple man—I knew him well, his name
was Jock Tibbets—he came to my yard and
died there of a fever, and his wife, why I
know not, she died also, so the two sons and
one daughter they did beg on the roads.
One of the sons was pressed to fight with
the king's men, and was killed; and the girl,
being but simple withal and miserably han-
dled by the soldiers, she was haired out of

her wits and drowned herself in the brook;
I saw her on the banks stark of her limbs,
and dripping, and her other brother making
moan over her."

"Yes," said the tapster, "Martin his
name is, and by the rood, Lord William be
going to hang him to-day, with our vicar."

"And how chance they hang him, sirrah?"
a voice demanded from within.

Guy had the curiosity to draw nearer
and look into the inn parlor. Two persons
were in the room. One was the speaker,
an elderly man, tall and stalwart of figure,
composed and benignant of face. His gray
hair was stiff and abundant. His features
were large and rather clumsily molded,
but the eyes were "marvelous bright,"
and wrinkles of kindly mirth discovered
themselves at the corners of his eyelids
and his mouth. His attire was "grave and
reverend" but plain, "a fair black gown"
and "black hose with ruffled plates of the
same cloth." Instead of the cap of the
period, he held a broad hat in his strong,
white hand.

"By the faith of my body, 'tis the bishop,"
said Guy.

The other person in the room was a
young gentlewoman, richly appareled, of
whose person the dim light only revealed
that she had a pale face and dark red hair.
But Guy did not need to see her plainly; he
had been fitting grand adjectives to that
auburn hair for months. Not much more
than two years before, Sir William Paget
had selected Mistress Margaret Carew for
his nephew's wife. There was "much
speech of the matter." The young people
saw each other. Mistress Margaret, a shy
girl, mourning the death of her mother, did
not so much as lift her eyes at the graceful
young cavalier, and blushed painfully at his
court flatteries. Guy was well enough satisfied; he told his uncle that the lady was fair
and that he would warrant her "infinitely
virtuous." "As for her wit," quoth he, "I
could wish it some growth, but there be
time enow."

Nevertheless the affair "came to naught."
I gather that there was some dispute about

"the dowry." Shortly after, Mistress Margaret married Sir John Godsalve.

Cotemporary gossip pictures Sir John as old, rich and ugly, a brave soldier and an honest if stormy tempered gentleman.

Guy took the rupture of his betrothal with equanimity; but when, after her marriage, Lady Godsalve appeared at court, whether because she were really grown more fascinating or because her charms had acquired the luster of the unattainable, certain it is Master Paget chose to fancy himself the victim of a hopeless passion. This was the period of his sonnets to Amoret.

Amoret was cold. She did not blush any for his compliments, and the wit, to which he had wished growth, was quite vigorous enough to match Master Guy's, now. He professed himself dying of despair, but I imagine that, at this period, there was a good deal of poetic license about his despair. At any rate, he consoled himself with kinder beauties. Guy was a man of his time, and it was not the time of Sir Galahad. Yet as he saw that averted pale cheek and the lovely curve of the throat into the cheek, he felt a thrill beyond his light admiration. "Dear child," he murmured, "Lord, what an innocent face it is!" All this was in the space of the tapster's gruff answer: "Why, please your lordship, Lord William willed Martin to hang our vicar, and he would not — so they are going to hang him — lo, there they come!"

A clatter of armor, a jingle of spurs, a thud of horses' hoofs, the rush of many feet, boys' feet, men's feet, women's feet, little children's feet, a troop of men-of-arms riding at a slow pace, and, in the middle rank, two men on horseback, arms tied behind their backs, feet lashed under their horses — yes, they were coming.

The priest's spine was as erect as any soldier's, though his robe bunched ungracefully over the saddle pommel, and they had tied a bucket of holy water, a rosary and a sacring bell round his neck, to splash and clank at every motion. He was a little round man with a bald head which glistened in the sun. He looked steadily at the tower and the beam, but he did not flinch by as much as the quiver of an eyelid; even his full cheeks kept their ruddy hue. The other prisoner was an athletic young man who would have been handsome but for the yellowish pallor of his skin and the glassy eyes which roamed from side to side. His curly flaxen hair was matted with blood, and his ragged fustian jacket nearly torn off him.

As the dismal procession moved up the street an inarticulate and awful murmur swelled from the crowd, that under-throb of rage and grief and straining patience that holds the menace of unchecked fury, and heard from an English mob has rarely failed to keep its promise. "Some day," thought the keen young interpreter who watched it all, "some day it will be the new priests' turn — ha, what meaneth my lord bishop?"

The bishop had stepped into the street. He stood there, lifting his arms

"My lord, in the king's name!"

The leader of the troop was a mere stripling well known to Guy, a duke's son.

He turned impatiently in his saddle, saying: "My lord, ye be letting the king's justice."

"Nay, not so," said the bishop, "sure, 'tis against the king's justice and natural pity, too, to hang this fond young man for that he will not hang the other."

Lord William answered, in a tone of impatient raillery, that the knave would hang the priest fast enough when the pinch came.

"That will I never," said the prisoner, sullenly.

The priest managed to turn his bound body toward the bishop. "For the passion of Christ, good gentlemen," he pleaded, "be a mean for this poor lad. 'Tis no rebel, but a poor miser that beggeth on the road."

"That will I, sir," said the bishop, heartily, "but for yourself —— "

"For me," said the priest, "pity me not. I have lived good days, and I am found worthy to die in God's cause."

Guy had been whispering in Lord William's ear, regarding the Protector's lenity toward the rebels. "He? He may want the like himself," said Lord William; but then he laughed and bade two of his soldiers "have the knave away."

"For the priest," he added, "I have no option."

The bishop thanked him for his "gentleness" and stepped aside. Lord William gave the word of advance. The troop moved on up the street, impassive as their armor. The people streamed after them, and, directly, Guy and the bishop saw the stout figure swinging before his own church tower. Lady Godsalve had gone. They stood alone together.

"God have pity on his soul!" said the bishop, solemnly; "he was a very pestilent traitor, well worthy of death, but he was a brave man."

Guy masked a pity that hurt him, under a careless answer: "Yea, he had a stout and arrogant stomach. He minded me of Forrest that was burned in the late king's time, ye know. I saw him suffer. You of the clergy have a special gift for torment, methinks. They burned him in a cradle of chains. Master Latimer preached, and at such length I trow Forrest was glad to be out of the sermon and into the fire. But, an he were not a traitor, I would say Forrest took his death as Christian-like as any man I ever did see. I was a lad, at the time. I wept to see the man, screaming in the fire, and climbing up, clinging to the chains, swaying his body out of the flames. Marry, I did run away."

The bishop sighed: "It liketh me not these harsh punishments, but they affright evil doers. Better is it one traitor die dreadfully like Forrest than hundreds in battle or — like such an one. But, Master Paget, ye have letters for me, I wis; let us to the green fields where we may read them in good quiet."

Guy willingly "did his bidding." They sat down together by the brookside and the bishop looked over the letters. They related to various abuses in the diocese, and especially to certain complaints privately made against the bishop. Their tenor appeared in the bishop's running comment: "Griffith ap Morgan be an unmeet man for promotion; he stole his own church bells. Canon Hugh Evans complaineth of the multitude of valyaunt beggars and sturdy vagabonds in his parish. The justice hath whipped and branded to no end; he would have two hanged as an ensample. Not an I can hinder it. Let him advise Sir Thomas Jones to open his mines; the poor lobs be willing enow to work so work be had. John Hughes! Nay, she was not his wife. I will not take bribes to bear with his wrong doing; let him complain. Ha! this be all false! It was not I, but George Constantine of his own presumptuous mind removed the communion altar in Caermarthen Church. Yea, it be very vile and in great decay. For why, the canons have spoiled it of crosses, censers, chalices with other plate and jewels to the value of five hundred marks. Your uncle hath the papers. I did take order to compel restitution. But they have bolsterers. I do perceive they make charges against me. Saw ye ever such frivole reasoning?" He smiled, although plainly distressed. "Here be a famous hotchpotch: Pemunire and using my clergy tyrannously, and wearing a *hat*—verily, there I must plead guilty, sith the proof be on me. It beareth off the cold in winter and the heat in summer, yet from the coil ye would deem a hat partook of the nature of mortal sin. Likewise I have had two godmothers for my son, 'making of his son a monster,' quoth they, 'and him a laughing stock.' Well, Master Paget, there were two wives being before at variance who desired both to be godmothers, so to make unity between them they were both received. What! complain they too that I whistle my child, saying that he understood my whistle when he was three days old, and so whistle him, daily, friendly admonition neglected — friendly forsooth! But 'tis true I do use with gravity all honest loving entertainment of the child to encourage him, thereafter, willingly to receive, at his father's mouth, wholesome doctrine of the true fear and love of God. It killeth my heart, Master Paget, to see how cruelly these innocents, that Christ loved, be entreated by their parents and masters. Marry, though, ye would laugh your fill, Master Paget, to see

Sam nigh leaping out of his mother's arms, hearing of my whistle, I not being in sight. The towardness of the babe, the nurse saith, is amazing — but I forget my canon's sore grief." He read with a mixture of sadness, vexation and humor a long list of charges almost incredible to the modern mind. The bishop did not forcibly take away the people's beads; he permitted them to "kneel and knock" to the sacrament. He seditiously wished, "speaking of the alteration of the coin," that "the penny should be in weight worth a penny of the same metal." He dined with his servants, and his talk was "not of godliness but of worldly matters." He neglected his books and preaching, and spent his time opening mines, surveying lands, and attending to fisheries. When he reached the last indictment the bishop wiped his brow. "God forgive me, sir," said he, "belike therein be a savor of truth. I be so occupied with the piteous condition for this world of my poor people and the seeking out some remede that I may neglect to feed my sheep spiritually, though I do preach regularly

every week. But Master Paget, enow of
this gear; ye bear your worshipful uncle's
very thought of the matter; pray you give
it me."

During the bishop's examination of the
letters Guy had been watching every
phrase, those sharp, worldly-wise young
ears of his on the alert for some ring
of the base metal of cruelty, or ambition, or
avarice, or sinister indulgence, which he
was used to detect in the "new priests'
talk."

"Almost thou persuadest me thou art an
honest man," he thought before he answered
courteously: "That will I, my lord. 'Tis
my uncle's belief the notary, George Constantine, is promoter of all this broil. 'Tis
bruited that he be not only guilty of theft
of church moneys and other naughty facts,
but he has had a hand in the late rising.
Wherefore, do ye inquire, shrewdly, and
secretly gather what proof ye may — it
needs not much — and hale him before Sir
Peter, who is your right friend and brother
— and there will be an end of him and his
plottings!"

"Mean ye," cried the bishop, opening his eyes wide, "mean ye that I have him hanged whether or no?"

Guy stroke the down on his smiling lip as he answered gently that the hanging best be left to the secular arm, that is, Sir Peter Carew.

"God forbid," said the bishop, flushing, "that I take any man's blood on my soul! I thank Sir William for his gentle friendship, but it standeth not with my honor or the faith of a Christian man thus to render evil for evil."

"Verily, 'tis an honest man," was Guy's inward comment; outwardly he said that his own duty ended with the delivery of his message. "And so the bishop put the papers in his poke and they fared back to the 'ostle."

Will, the tapster, met them with a grin and the intelligence: "Martin, him your worships wot of"—he griped his throat significantly—"he hath led the soldiers into a ditch and is off."

"Another knave to pillage the king's lieges," said Guy, tossing the fellow a cru-

sado and secretly rather glad. He suspected that the bishop shared his feeling.

The evening was spent in the parlor of
the inn. Mistress Ferrars was present, a
tall, slender gentlewoman, neither young
nor pretty, yet attracting by a mild and un-
exacting comeliness and an evident sweetness of nature.

Lord William contributed his handsome
person and his sackbut, "playing divers
French songs most untunefully"—but this
is Guy's judgment, and he wanted to en-
gross Lady Godsalve's attention himself.
He was too courtly a youth to display his
chagrin; he rather made extra efforts to
please the whole company. He discoursed
on the doings of the court, the dress of the
ladies at the last masque; the new salad just
come from France; the beauty, talents and
marvelous virtues of the young prince
(whereat the bishop's eyes grew moist and
he nodded his head "many times in a vehe-
ment manner," and was heard to murmur
something in his wife's ear about "our
Sam"); the fair gardens of the Duke of
Somerset; the wonders of France, Holland

and Italy, which countries young Paget had seen with his uncle.

The simple pair delighted in this talk. Ever and anon the bishop would turn his beaming eyes at his wife and they would smile in unison upon Guy. He caught his breath with interest over the foreign marvels, and laughed a great, round, unclerical laugh at every jest. Finally, when Guy sang at his asking (the rascal abused his opportunity and adapted some of his own ravings about "Amoret" to a "fair foreign melody") he rubbed his eyes, openly, exclaiming: "Tush, I had not thought a fond song could so move me. Thou must teach it me, that I may whistle it to Sam."

Guy could not help an expansion of his heart under this artless admiration. But when the conversation touched on the state of the commonwealth he was impressed with the sturdier side of Ferrars's character. A homely acumen edged his straightforward sentences. His mind had a breadth of justice and mercy, and a fanciful imagination as well, which played about his stern honesty and blunt courage, just as little

Sam used to frolic in his father's arms and rest his dainty cheek against the other's wrinkles.

"Yea, verily, here is an honest man," said Guy to himself.

While the company sate about the room and Lord William explained the last campaign to the bishop, and Mistress Ferrars was counting her stitches on a remarkable sampler, he made an occasion to go to Lady Godsalve, to examine her broidery work, saying (which was not true) that it minded him of a piece worked by the Lady Mary, the king's sister. So he leaned over the gable of her chair and his fingers slipped along the silken pattern until they touched the slim white fingers drawing the thread. He audaciously asked her how she liked the song. "'Twas writ for you," said he.

Lady Godsalve folded her hands upon her work. "Master Paget," she said, "I would fain talk with you in good sadness if I might."

"Assuredly, madam," Guy answered, perplexed by her calm voice and the steady gaze of her eyes. Then, all at once, he saw that her hands were clasping each other with the tightness of resolution, not self-control. She lifted her eyes. They were long in shape, and not until she lifted them did one see how large they were or how deep their violet lights. Faint shadows lay under her smooth eyelids. Her eyebrows, darker than her hair, were drawn a little together. The small mouth curved downward the merest trifle. It was the short upper lip, Guy could see, that gave the mouth its haughty expression; now, the lips had the pathetic curves of the mouth of a tired child. Surely her cheek had grown thinner and paler.

Guy recalled the girl who should have been his wife and who was "infinitely virtuous." He was touched. All the artificial gallantry slipped from his manner; he stood up and held the embroidery in both his hands as if to examine it.

She gave him the first grateful look that he had ever seen in her eyes. "Master Paget," she went on, hurriedly, "brought ye news of the accusations Constantine, the notary, hath laid against the bishop?"

"Alack, madam, my matters be private."

"Nay, it needs not you disclose them," she said, with rather a dreary smile. "I wot 'tis true withouten your speech. Ah, Master Paget, be his good lord. Intercede with your uncle. He be not a clawback flatterer like his besetters; he cannot plead his own cause. He hath done so much in Wales for the poor people. And he hath taken order with the misbehaving clergy; therefore they do hate him, and practice to destroy him."

"He hath good hap to win such an advocate," said Guy, smiling a little.

"He hath done more for me," she answered; "once when I was in sore trouble and anguish of mind, seeing no helper, he set my feet in the straight road; and his counsel was like the ropes they do throw to poor mariners in a storm. He looketh a kind, simple man only, but oh, he doth know the depths wherein the soul be like to sink!"

During her words the young courtier's heart was beating in an unprecedented way. Could Margaret Godsalve's extremity concern him? That still damsel who scarce let him see the color of her eyes, had she loved him in secret? Poor heart, to have them rudely fling her sweetness at that brutal old soldier! Was her flouting of him but to hide her hurt? Guy recalled his sonnets. He was smitten with the sharpest regret that he had ever known; his seemed to him an unknightly part, and he remembered his mother and her tales of knights who loved one woman and clave to her and served her, asking no guerdon.

"Margaret," said he, "forget what hath given thee pain in time agone. I will be thy right brother, now. Whatever I can do, that will I; wherefore, thou knowest, but shalt never hear me say."

He had spoken to her thought rather than her words, but neither of them considered that until afterward. She was anything but pale, now; she turned her face so that he might not see the blushes—so like those blushes when they were first together—her sweet voice was barely above a whisper: "I knew, always, thou wast noble—as noble as thou art brave!"

She might have added something to these intoxicating words; but Lord William was moved to ask her "a fool question."

The following morning Guy rode back to London. He tells that he made the journey, "heavily revolving many things in his mind." He did not know it, but he had passed through a momentous experience: at one and the same time he had been awakened to his best impulses as a citizen and as a man. He had his crude and cynical imaginations of man and woman jostled out of shape; for in Ferrars he found an honest married priest, and in the insolently adored mistress of his fancy, the woman whom he should love all the days of his life.

If there was one being Guy despised more than another it was "the married priest." This opinion was the common property of his time; even the Princess Elizabeth could not rid herself of it, and when one reads the published defense of their marriages given the world by some of the English clergy, it may be owned that the scornful had some excuse. Guy himself, like a multitude of young Englishmen of his generation, buffeted backward and forward between Catholicism and Protestantism, was, in the phrase of the time, "a neuter, a person of no faith." To him the new religion looked an indecent scramble for spoils on the part of the laity, and for license on the part of the clergy; and the married priests with their wives and children and their greedy palms were a noxious and scandalous spectacle. Yet today he had seen a married priest who loved his wife and child, and none the less had kept clean hands and a pure heart. That Ferrars was not of the exalted spiritual type, but simply a healthy, not too refined follower of righteousness, helped his influence over Guy, who had the moderate man's incredulous contempt for exaltation of feeling.

"I will never maintain again that a new priest may not be a true man," said Guy.

And he has left his own record of his state of mind regarding Margaret.

"Before, when he was assured she regarded him not, he had pursued her right earnestly; but now that he did perceive that

she had bestowed her heart upon him (so un-
worthy) he was mazed and durst no longer
proceed, but would as it were protect her,
yea against his own self. So was he sore
distraught, seeing no joy or delight in living
without this lady; yet fully persuaded she
would in no wise fall from her duty to her
lord ; and, therewith consumed with such
excess of admiring and longing sorrow that
he did weep to think of her, yet could he
by no manner of means divert his mind
from her."

Edward was dead and Mary reigned in
his stead, and the mass was back in England, before Guy saw the little Devonshire
town again.

Meanwhile evil days had come to Robert
Ferrars. So long as Somerset was in
power, the Pagets' influence kept his enemies at bay; but Sir William's address
only availed to save his own neck, after the
duke's fall. He retired to what was left of
his estates, and Guy went to help fight the
Turks. Presently, Ferrars was summoned
to London on the same "frivole reasonings"

which he had discussed with Guy. He was thrown into prison, and in prison he was, on Mary's accession to the throne. The Pagets came back with the Catholic queen. The Lord Paget had been the most moderate of Protestants; he was an equally tolerant Catholic; but moderate men were speedily pushed into the background by fanatics wild with the unslaked hatreds of the time.

In vain all Guy's influence was exerted for the bishop's release. He was deposed from his see as a married priest; he was kept in prison. His wife sickened and died, but Guy obtained the poor boon of taking him, under his own charge, for a farewell visit to her. There is still extant an affecting letter which the bishop wrote to Margaret Godsalve relating to this visit. And with the bishop's letter is one of thanks to Guy from Margaret—evidently inclosing the first. Margaret's letter is indorsed in Guy's handwriting: "My Dearling Lady, Her first letter writ to Me."

Margaret at this point was in France. Her father had been concerned in Wyatt's insurrection and fled. Her husband, though nominally loyal to the queen, was reported to sympathize secretly with the insurgents.

It is written in every history how Lord Paget succeeded in defeating the heresy bills of two parliaments, and how he failed in the third. In every history, also, is it written how, though he failed when the question only touched men's lives, he succeeded at every point in keeping for the laymen all the church property which Henry VIII had stolen for them. Naturally, all this did not help Paget's court favor. He remained president of the Welsh Marshes. He was of her majesty's privy council. The lands which had been confiscated were his again. But the queen looked coldly on him; he was " vehemently suspect," and "my Lord of Winchester did whisper to my Lord Riche at the Lady Jane's execution that, for a small pretext, they would make the Lord Paget's head dance the like dance."

Shortly after, Guy, being summoned by his uncle, found that cool-headed statesman "in a fume."

"By God's wounds, nephew Guy," were the first words Guy could win, "these bloody tikes of priests will break the neck of mother church, of their own swinge! Ten heretics burned in this one month! They be the veriest dolts! Wot they not 'tis the best of the new religion will stand steadfast, and men will pity their sufferings, and, at the length, turn on their tormenters! By the passion of Christ, it putteth me out of my patience! And now they will send the poor old age, Master Ferrars, down to Wales to be tried of the new bishop, Morgan, and that cursed knave, Constantine. An he do not recant—and ye wot he is of stomach stout and hard — they will sure burn him. They did send him down to Wales with Lord William Radcliffe ; but they need *him* elsewhere, so they demanded me, in the council this morning, if ye were not trusty to be sent.' I ween 'tis to practice with us that they may find a pretext to destroy us; but I durst not refuse.

"Thou must go, Guy. See to it the man doth not give ye the slip, and that he be

mercifully entreated.   God, He knoweth I
do rue for him."

So, "very heavily," Guy went.   He had
planned a different errand to Devonshire.
Sir John was dead and Margaret, he had
heard, was in England again.   Of what had
been his relations with Lady Godsalve during the intervening years; whether he had
ever tried to drag his star from heaven,
whether he had kept his own fidelity un-
stained through all the temptation of his
youth and that unbridled time — of such
matters Guy has said nothing, but it is
plain that Margaret was still "infinitely
virtuous" as she was infinitely fair; and
the stiff phrases of the day relax into grace
and tenderness if they do but approach her
image.

Therefore, not only "marvelous sorrowful" over Ferrars's sad case, but "much
afeared lest the lady might take his errand
in ill part," Guy rode into Devonshire to
the same village where he had encount-
ered Lord William before.   There was
little change in the aspect of the village
street.   The church had plain windows,

and a priest in a white rochet was celebrating mass, while a bell tolled from the tower before which stout Sir Giles had swung. He was welcomed at the inn by the landlady, grown a trifle weightier and rosier, and by Will tapster, himself, standing now in the landlord's shoes, that timorous worthy having escaped to the only sure refuge from tumult and fear in England, the village graveyard.

The porch seats were filled much as they had been before, and the rustics stared at the soldiers' corselets and hacquebuts with the same mixture of dread and aversion. Guy made out some of the faces; but the young man who had praised Latimer was gone. The hostess had kept all the details of his visit with rural tenacity, and recalled them volubly. She had not lost her habit of bold speech. "Well a day, 'tis rare good luck your worship be come," she cried; "Lord William he be reveling with a great sort of gentlemen at the hall, and the poor old heretic man been put in a little blind house adjoining, where we do keep the coals; and no fire withal, so he be like to starve for cold!"

Laying up a reckoning (which he afterward paid in full) for Lord William, in his own mind, Guy had Ferrars removed to the inn chamber, where was a fire and a supper laid out, and the best bed well warmed.

The bishop, who had greeted Guy with all his usual affection, now looked about him with a broad smile. "Yea, even pennar and inkhorn!" he exclaimed, gleefully. "Verily, good youth, thou art my white son. God be praised, 'tis in dolour and hardness that a man findeth out the kindness of men. The good man of the house he did fet me a great mess of meat and bread and a stoup of wine; and the woman did send me the cloak of her husband that dead is. He was of slight personage," the bishop laughed, "and I as ye see, but, marry, it softened the coals for me, and I have an ill back. I pray you, Sir Guy, thank her for her gentleness. The keepers in the city left me little, but I have a silver groat I would send her."

"This is not the meeting I had hoped

for," groaned Guy, unmanned by the old man's cheerfulness.

"Nay, good youth, thou hast done thine uttermost for me; regret it not, nor rue for me.   I mind me ever of the old saying:

> ' Although the day be ever so long
> At last it ringeth to evensong. '

Pray you sup with me, my son, and tell me of our friends."

Then followed a scene strange enough, but of a like nature to those witnessed often in England, at this time.

The heretic and his most unwilling guard supped together while the soldiers watched outside.   Vainly the courtier taxed his subtle wit to persuade Ferrars to choose life instead of death.

"Oh, consider," he cried, unconsciously speaking the words of another man of the world to a martyr, "life is sweet and death is bitter; and will ye die for such empty words?"

A very pleasant, gentle smile stole over the old man's rugged features, gaunt and pale with imprisonment. "Ye remember," said he, "I was ever addict to songs

and rhymes. My dear heart, when she was
with me, did often repeat to me one that
marvelously comforted me:

'He that dieth with honor liveth forever,
But the defaméd dead recovereth never.'

Nay, nay, my son, I die for no idle words,
but for the very truth of God."

"Ye would die against the mass, and
poor Father Giles he died for the mass,"
said Guy with the irritation of despair;
"ye cannot both be right —— "

"Nay, Father Giles be all wrong," said
the bishop, cheerily, "I have the warrant
of Holy Writ."

Thus the talk went on as such talk was
going on in England, whenever the man of
the world and the man of the other world
held their everlasting dispute. Guy was
too shrewd not to perceive the helplessness
of his arguments. He was as powerless to
move the bishop as the bishop would have
been to persuade the young courtier to go
to the stake on his own account because he
did not believe in the "mummery of the
mass."

Sadly enough he bade the old man good-night and betook himself to his chamber. He had posted his guards about the house and he made the rounds before he retired. Down the street the flare of the torches showed him three soldiers. "Those be Lord William's antients, belike," said the old lieutenant who had served with Paget in Hungary. Just then one of them turned his head. Guy experienced that undefined sense of recognition which often bothers the man trained to remember faces. "Somewhere did I see that fellow's hawk eyes," thought Guy.

His troops placed, the chamber where the bishop lay guarded at every approach, Guy went into the porch chamber which was his own. The porch chamber was built out from the house above the porch, a common architectural feature in Tudor mansions. Leaning out of the window, he could plainly hear the voices of the loiterers in the porch. Guy extinguished his taper and listened. It was more to distract his thoughts than from any analyzed purpose.

Now and then a sentence rose above the murmur.

"Well, I care not for strangers, gaffer; but poor Jock Dobson —— "

"He be a right merciful man an he do be a heretic. I did see him beg Martin's life i' this very place."

"Martin, forsooth! 'twas an ill fact that — 'tis the most arrant rogue and robber i' the country side."

"Never a soul i' this town hath had wrong of Martin."

The words were lost in an unintelligible buzz of Martin's exploits, besprinkled with peals of laughter as if Martin's wickedness must have a humorous twang. Then some voice said that Martin had seen "the heretic."

"Say, dame," was the next clear sentence, "will they burn him like they did poor Dobson?"

"Yea, but not here, they only bide here overnight. They will burn him in Wales. Alack the pity, 'tis a hard death, burning!"

"The gospelers be in some sort Christian men"—Guy recognized the mercer's voice—"I think burning should be for ana-baptists and arians and such like."

"I warrant I could not abide the fire. I should recant."

"Best not take up with their gay glorious doctrines, then, gossip; they be all of the devil, Father Giles said."

"Marry, this same Lord William was 't that hanged him; then would he give the mass ne cap ne knee; and he hacked the rood down and made a gallows out o't for to hang a poor good Catholic clown. How chance he hath not been dealt roundly with? This poor man did no burning, no hanging that I wot of; yet Lord William hath lands and lordship, but this poor miser needs burn. Neighbors, I be the queen's right subject, God bless her; but I like not these burnings."

"The times be no better," an aged voice grumbled, "and there be a meanie of Spanish men to eat up all poor England hath. 'Tis bruited the queen meaneth to make the prince king, for the great love she hath for him."

"More than he for her, belike," the yeoman muttered.

No one reproved him; they were suddenly

all so silent that Guy looked down the street
for the cause, instantly apparent in the approach of several figures on horseback.
Coming under the light from the inn windows they were revealed as a gentlewoman,
an old serving woman, and two serving men,
all attended by Guy's lieutenant and half a
dozen soldiers.

"I seek Sir Guy Paget, good people,"
said a voice that made his pulses bound. In
a moment he was before the lady of his
dreams. She was calm enough; every other
emotion had been smothered by the stress
of one overwhelming fear.

"Sir Guy, thou knowest mine errand without my telling it. Thou hast mine uncle's
life in thy hands. Oh, be his good lord!"

"Alas, madam, I have no power," said Guy;
"I have labored him sore to recant, but he
will not."

"And there be no hope for him with Morgan and Constantine," said the lady, "I know
that right well."

Guy assented, despondently.

"How wicked be these laws," she cried,
wringing her hands, but dry-eyed in her

misery; "an I were a man I would fight them till I died!"

"My uncle, he did his uttermost in parliament," said Guy, feeling the weakness of his words. He could not keep his eyes away from her, where she stood, the candle-light on her white face and her curling dark red hair and glittering eyes and the scarlet, trembling lips.

"In parliament! like clerks!" the passionate speech flowed on, "but ye be a valiant knight, ye wear a sword. Think, they will burn twenty this week! Some of them be women, some lads, nigh children, that never *heard* of any other religion. How can the nobles and gentles of England sit by and see such foul shame!"

"What profiteth fighting?" said Guy. "Wyatt, what hath he done to help the heretics? He hath only lost his own head and many an honest gentleman's beside." He caught the hands that she flung up in a wild gesture, and held the white wrists. "Listen, dear heart—nay, ye shall not scorn me, Margaret, I be no coward knave, my heart is heavy for these poor heretics. Yea, I would *fight* for them, did fighting serve ; but the Lady Mary is our rightful queen. I will not bring in the French king to con-quer England."

She let her face droop until her cheek rested almost against his hands which were holding her wrists. " Forgive me, Sir Guy, I did wrong thee. Alack, I be haired out of my wits with the planning and thinking. I know thou wouldst serve him. And it is so easy. Ah, sir, do for me one little, little thing?"

"What, sweetheart?" he said, dreamily. How passing sweet it was to have her so near him—and she was free!

" The password for to-night."

She whispered in his ear, "Just that—only that —to me."

"What would ye with the password?"

"Nay, do not ask.   Best to know naught. Only tell it me."

" 'Tis a device to free Master Ferrars."

He spoke very gently but sadly. Suddenly he kissed her wrist.

"Thou knowest how I love thee," he

groaned, "and thou wouldst make me a forsworn man!"

"Nay, not so. Leave holding of my
hands, Sir Guy, I pray thee."

When he dropped her wrists she turned
and sat down, making a piteous effort at
composure. "Fy, I do talk like a fond woman. Look, I will go to work roundly with
you to amend your reasoning. Prythee
allow me require certain things of ye. Is
it because ye deem this law to be righteous
that ye help it thus, or because ye be sent
to execute it?"

"Ye wot 'tis the latter. I be a soldier. I
obey them that have authority."

"But deem ye a soldier must obey always? Say they command ye murder babes,
like King Herod? Or like him that sent to
kill the babes in the Tower? Did those
slayers, by authority, right well? Or say,
the queen—the which is a shrewd likelihood, sith she be a cruel and irous dame—
say she will ye to despatch the Lady Elizabeth? Shall ye do her will and wash your
hands, saying, 'Marry, I be sent by authority'? Tush! Away with such reasoning for

a free-born Englishman! I tell ye, Sir Guy Paget, ye stain your knightly sword when ye lift it in such a quarrel! He is a gentleman that hath gentle conditions. And he that helpeth wicked men to murder—and, lo! how cruelly!—an innocent, kind old man that hath wrought only good, yea, by God's mercy, he be no gentleman, no knight, but a murdering slave!"

"Ye drive me too hard," cried the young man, beside himself; "I tell ye, my uncle, that is more than a father to me, he hath my word. Oh, Margaret, show pity, drive me not out of my manhood!"

But she was too much of a woman to be merciful. She rose. She walked to him and knelt at his feet.

"Guy," she whispered, while he could hardly see her face for the daze of anguish in his eyes, "Guy, often hast thou sworn that thou lovest me; and I could not tell thee how even so did I love thee. No one will know; Martin (he that the bishop saved, here, in this town) will do all. Thy uncle will have no guilt. *Thou* need'st know nothing or—" she lifted her radiant eyes to him—"thou shalt know *all* and fly with him—and me—to my father in Normandy. My father will not refuse me to thee—*then!*"

How many times had Guy pictured this moment when he should speak his heart and know hers; he had hoped and trembled, he had conjured up a hundred possibilities, but never—never anything like this. In his deep bitterness of soul he groaned aloud.

And with that, "seeing him so moved and being in a measure distraught with her misery, she did embrace his feet with weeping tears, calling him her dear lord, and such like expressions, which did, as it were, sear his heart; so that he was marvelous fain to give her her will, yet would he not yield."

It could not be, he said; he had given his word to his uncle.

She urged him further, for she knew that the lieutenant of the guard was to come directly; imploring him if he decided for mercy to send a ring ("therewith she gave it him") by Will tapster, "who was trusty," with the password written and slipped into a hiding place in the ring.

Scarcely had she shown him the "trick of the stone" before the lieutenant's knock was heard.

They had but a moment together. Margaret drew Guy's dark head down until it was level with her eyes. She kissed him. "That do I," she said, while he looked at her "like a dumb man with a knife in his heart," "because after this night either thou art my husband, or else a man barbarous and forsworn whom I never will see more—and I have loved thee as mine own soul!"

She dropped her hands and opened the door. Guy saw her step into the shadows, he heard the rustle of her gown on the floor. She turned and passed down the stair.

"Come back to me when I call," Guy told the lieutenant; "I have somewhat to write, before."

He closed the heavy door upon the man. He was left alone with his dilemma.

To Martin's plans he had no clew—nor does he supply any to us out of his later knowledge—but he felt sure, now, that the

soldier with the vaguely recognized face
was the outlaw himself.

Martin may have contemplated strategy
alone; but it is likely he had force in reserve.
The burning of Dobson and two others of
the townspeople had seriously shaken their
loyalty. Martin was sure of their tacit good
will. Armed with the password, he could
introduce his men into the inn. If the queen's
men resisted, there would be bloody fighting and the bishop would be "conveyed
away" in the *mêlée*. "Then will the poor
knaves lose their lives because I have first
lost mine honor," thought Guy, bitterly.
"And what would befall his uncle while he
led a merry life with his wife in France?"

All his life, Guy had not only loved his
uncle, he had also admired that long-headed
and rather cool-hearted courtier, above all
living men. Apart from any question of
soldierly duty or his conduct as a subject,
his defection would most probably ruin Sir
William. On the other hand, was he to be
the minister of a hideous injustice, to de-
liver the affectionate and brave old man, to
whom he owed the awakening and purify-

ing of his own soul, over to the most cruel of deaths, and to lose forever his most precious hopes? Let him describe the conflict in his own words: "Wherefore I was in anguish and tumult of soul, thinking whether it be best to quit my allegiance and my faith to my uncle who trusted me ever with all he had, or whether to both be the cause of a good man's destruction and to lose her that was dearest to me of any woman in the world, I being then a young man at an age over which Love hath his extremest power."

He paced the floor. At times he wrung his hands, at times he wept; but in the end he summoned his lieutenant and bade him prepare all things for departure. He wrote a letter to Margaret explaining his course and its harsh necessity. This letter he sent to her (with the ring) by Will tapster. "And by this time, all being in readiness, they fared forth on their journey."

There is a large space devoted to the journey into Wales, in Guy's narrative. He described the doomed man's "joyance" in the sunshine, in the spring green creeping into the sedges and covert sides, in the flight of the herons, the song of the mavis, and the crisp air; "he having been so long pent away from all." He tells how people used to stand at the wayside to see them pass, "most often of sad countenance, and many crying: 'God sustain you, sir!' or 'God send you deliverance!'"

He repeats all Ferrars's affecting talk of his son, and his messages to the child, and his own promise to "deal with the little Samuel like as it were his own son." He gives the "jests" and the "stories" and the "merry quips on words" in which the old man indulged, after the fashion of his time; as well as the grave and godly talk. But it would seem that in his last days, as always, Ferrars had more faith in doing justice and showing mercy than in spiritual exercises; though he humbly reproaches himself therefor, "with dullness and grossness of nature and over love of this glosing world." Guy has not omitted a touch in the picture; he cannot bear to slight a word of this man who moves him so strongly and whom he had given over to death. We can see the cheery old man on Guy's own fiery charger ("for as old as he been there was no horse he could not ride, and all beasts loved him ") whistling the notes of the birds or "godly tunes."

"For sure," said he, "it were ungrateful to the Lord that granteth me these days of solace before my trial not to joy in them and strengthen my heart. The Lord loveth a *cheerful* giver, be it of life or gear."

But Guy, himself — one only finds here and there a hint of his confused misery.

They had reached the Welsh marshes when they were overtaken by a flying horseman. He delivered to Guy, as token, the ring which he had such sorrowful cause to know, and a pacquet. The pacquet contained a letter to Ferrars and another to himself. When he opened the latter he found only his own eager words of pleading and pain.

The town of Caermarthen is the principal town of the diocese of St. Davids. It lies on the river Towy, and its narrow streets creep up a hill to the market place and the massive castle, old as the Welsh

princes. On the thirty-first day of March,
1555, the market place had but one vacant
spot, a little space about the cross, in which
a four-cornered pile of fagots had been built
as high as a man's waist. An oaken stake
stood in the center and a chain was locked
to the stake.

Like a wide wall of light the sunshine
shifted from blazing point to point of breast-
plates, steel caps and halberts, massed
close as men could stand between the stake
and the wavering, black sea of Welsh hats
and frieze. A platform had been erected,
whereon, as the custom was, the priests
and commissioners sate, to watch the hideous pageant. People pointed out a sleek,
dark-skinned priest nervously fidgeting his
arms in his wide velvet sleeves; and the
name Constantine passed from mouth to
mouth.

On the platform they "bore a solemn
countenance," relaxed now and then when
some wag told a good story such as in our
day would beguile the tedium of the pall
bearers' ride to the grave.

But below, among the pale women and

men with set jaws and lowering brows, and the little children who had loved Robert Ferrars, the suffering whom he had comforted and the friendless poor whom he had defended, there was no jesting. Tears were on many faces. One man standing close to the guards could not wipe his eyes because he was holding a bag of gunpowder, and a soldier near by did him that office, his own eyes full. Presently this soldier was holding the bag, and the man had disappeared.

The crowd have waited since dawn, and it is now noon; but no one goes away. Mothers ease the children's blistered feet by holding them in their arms.

Now a universal movement in the crowd shakes a little even that burnished line of steel. Every head is turned to the little group coming slowly from the castle gateway. Taller than any of them, all the people recognize that well loved figure and the familiar hat. Before they reach the market place a haggard rider on a flagging horse gallops through the lane made for him at once. There are cheers and shouts of "Grace! grace!" "A pardon! a pardon!"

"There be no grace, good people, only the devil's wonted bait!" shouts a strong voice; and a wail in women's tones echoes the bold heretic.

Guy has not heard them at all. He is so spent with his long ride and the sleepless nights, before, that he tumbles off his saddle at Master Ferrars's feet. "Ha, good youth," says the kind, loud voice Guy knows, "the Lord be praised I see ye once more."

Guy knows that Margaret is close to him, and, clinging to her, a fair haired child; but he has no power to feel an additional pang; he knows that Margaret must have told the bishop all; but he has no feeling left to be hurt or comforted by the serene and kindly gaze that is bent on him.

He takes out a paper and makes the last ineffectual appeal. He felt it useless when he started, but to make it he has ridden night and day. The paper is the mildest possible form of recantation. Let the bishop sign it, no public penance shall be exacted; he shall be free to leave the country.

So Guy tells him, and the sheriff adds his word of persuasion, being a merciful man.

Every one near can hear the bishop's answer. "Consider, fair sir, how thou, a neuter and a worldly person, would not break thy faith to thine earthly lord, but would rather be letted of a great estate and of the wife thou hast chosen; then shall I, for the sake of a few more years or the queen's favor, forsake my good God? Nay, God helping me, never. If death come, welcome be it. True, the manner of it be dreadful, but it is the portal to life eternal." Then smiling he added: "'Tis like thou, beholding, wilt suffer more than I; so, as a sign that the pain be bearable I will hold up my hands." Guy entreated him no more. He saw him embrace his child, who cried a little at the crowd and the sad faces, and did not understand why he might not go with his father; but was led away smiling, at last, with Margaret's gold chain.

The muscles of the father's face quivered, and he dashed his hand across his eyes. "A good child, and winsome," he said, in a husky voice. "Ye will remember, Sir Guy."

Then he embraced Guy and blessed him, and so went cheerfully on to his suffering.

It was long told in Wales how the brave old man lifted his hands, nor once stirred them, amid the flames.

Guy heard the crash of powder.

Then he ventured to look; but still the intrepid hands were lifted.

A groan of horror and pity burst from the crowd. "Put fire! set to fire!" yelled the sheriff. They did not have time to obey him; a bill hook, wielded by a hand too merciful to falter, caught the spring sunshine on its edge as it swang; the gray head sank, and there was no more need for courage or for pity. The man with the bill flung it down and sobbed. Sick at heart, Guy crawled away. He sat down in the shadow of the gateway and abandoned himself to his grief.

A hand was laid lightly on his arm, but not even when he saw the white face and the woeful, tearless eyes could he realize that Margaret had come to him.

"He hath sent me," she said; "Oh, God forgive you, Guy, I am his last gift to you!"

As the years dulled emotion I suppose that Margaret came to forgive her husband —even, perhaps, to understand his conduct; but whenever I look at the picture and the smile that has so little mirth, so deep an experience, I query in my own mind: Did Guy ever decide if he acted right, or was he only sure that as grim a perplexity would have awaited him on the other side of the dilemma?

But our honest Martin always maintained that my lord did act fair and honest, since having passed his word he kept it. "Like I kept mine to the lady Margaret," said Martin. "And sure 'twas a right comfort that my lord was able to give the knave Constantine his deserts and he died in prison."

Martin, be it understood, was a reformed man at this speaking. The narrative tells naïvely that so great was the effect of Ferrars's death on him "that he did straight forsake his evil courses, and sailing over seas, he commenced buccaneer with Sir Peter Carew."

His reformed ways prospered to such an extent that he was knighted by Queen Elizabeth, and, retiring on the spoils of his reformation, became a model country gentleman and one of the soundest and most regular sleepers of the parish church.

I fancy if Lord Ellesmere went to church he did not sleep. I imagine him smiling as the crude commonplace dragged along, seeing perhaps the kind, strong, childlike face of another preacher, drearily pondering on that never ending dilemma.

But little Samuel grew up happily; and never knew why sometimes his benefactor's hand was laid so tenderly on his head and Lord Ellesmere sighed.

The Court of Last Resort

The Court of Last Resort.

'Tis a poor thing, but mine own.—Shakespeare.

DOROTHY LAWRENCE, looking one summer day from the veranda of "the big house," saw the ferry toiling across the Black river. The ferryman paddled slowly, for the current is swift. The passengers were a woman and boy, both black, in a white-covered "mover's wagon."

They had already reached the shore when the oxen became frightened, with the stupid strong fright of their kind; and a clamor of shouts, a vast waving of the paddle, and backing and stumbling of the oxen ended in the wagon's being dumped in the river.

Here the woman emerged from the wagon. Coolly dropping her dress skirt on the seat, she jumped into the water after the oxen. Waist high in the green waves, she swung her whip and shouted at the brutes exactly as if on dry land, finally driving them in good order up the bank. Then she disappeared behind the wagon, to emerge again, dry and clad.

"There is a sensible darky!" thought Dorothy, who by this time was making ready to go to the store for her husband. The store was only a stone's throw from the house, but Colonel Lawrence liked to have his wife come toward supper time and walk home with him; after ten years of married life, the Lawrences were still in love with each other. As Dorothy strolled under the shade of the row of gum trees, she looked at the wagon, which stood by itself, with the oxen loose and the pole on the ground. The oxen were fat, well-conditioned beasts. The wagon had a new top and was painted a bright red of an uneven gloss, that, with the absence of decorating hair lines and such bedizenments, suggested the home artist. A large Arkansas hound slept under the wagon bed. Inside, one could see the swelling outlines of a feather bed, sacked in burlap, the corner of a covered sewing machine, and a cooking stove. Plainly, this was a mover of means.

The little boy was playing near the wagon. He might be nine years old, a little brown creature whose cheeks dimpled continually. All the buttons were on his shirt, and his short trousers were new and clean.

The woman had walked toward the store. Colonel Lawrence came down the steps and she addressed him. He beckoned to his wife to join him, which she did, perceiving that here was one of the times that he preferred facing in company. She could see that he was listening to a tale of wrong, for he nodded his head and pulled at his black moustache, frowning at intervals, and murmured: "Hmn! hmn!" in the vague and non-committal sympathy of the man who must listen to the complaints of many.

"So Jake Willis is your husband," were the first words that Dorothy heard, "and you parted ——"

"No, sah," eagerly interrupted the woman, "we ain't done pahted. He run away wid Lize Ma'y Hunter. I never did give nare consent, sah!"

The colonel recognized the distinction — a "parting," among the negroes, being a mutual ceremony. There are negotiations and solemn division of the property and a semi-legal severance of the marriage bonds.

"I see," said Colonel Lawrence; "you didn't agree. And you want him back?"

"Dat's it, boss—yes, sah; Jake, he did prommus me solemn, las' time, he won't never run 'way agin. Now, sah, will you please kin'ly have Jake turn dat nigger loose an' come off back wid me, or let me go 'long er him, jes' what he wantster; I ain't aimin' to be ha'sh wid Jake! He kin have his ruthers consarnin' dat p'int!"

While the woman talked — she spoke in a low, mellow voice, with neither hurry nor excitement in the liquid notes — Dorothy was looking her over. There was something to look over, it may be said, since the deserted wife was nearly five feet ten inches in height, and, though not stout, of a square and ample build. She had not the fatal gift of beauty, being of the genuine coal-black, flat-nosed, Nubian type of negro, and having cross-eyes to the bargain; but there was something attractive in her exceptional tidiness of dress and in the anxious good humor of her countenance, and something almost graceful in her perfect command of every muscle as she moved.

"She is not quite the ordinary darky," thought Dorothy.

The colonel chewed the ends of his moustache and frowned, signs of perplexity recognized by his wife.

"Well, you see, Mrs. Willis," said he, "I don't know much about Jake; he came here with a woman that he calls his wife, representing that they were just married, and took seventy-five acres on the yon side of the creek. I don't know when he will be down to the store."

"Dat 's all right, sah; I seen Jake a-settin' on de steps of de sto', when I come 'cross de river."

"You say this girl isn't his wife?" The colonel saw he could not postpone the question, and braced himself with an audible sigh.

"Dat she ain't, sah," said the woman; "she ben Sol Hunter's wife, but he died up.

She got him to paht from his wife, she done so; and she done make her brags dat she wud git Jake 'way from me 'fo' Christmas. She sayed as how Jake done runned away afo', and he knowed de way!"

"Oh, he ran away before, did he?"

"Yes, sah; it ben like dis: we-uns got a fyarm down Memphis way, nigh 'bout paid fo'; and, come time fo' de morgige, we got de money tergedder. Jedge Covington, he lent us hunderd dolla's, an' we got de restis — dat 's hunderd an' forty-two, 'cause I did make dat up wid de crap an' de aigs and de claybank colt we sole. An' I ben a plum' idjit an' let Jake fetch de money from de jedge — two hunderd an' forty-two dolla's, sah — and Jake, he did feel so peart and gaily dat he jest ben obleeged, it look like, to stop at de cross-roads sto' fo' to git a drink; and dar he met up wid two wicked niggers from a boat, an' dey got him to playin' of craps. Well, sah, 'fo' dat fool Jake cud bat his eye, 'most, dem niggers got all his money plumb 'way from him. So Jake, he does be mighty tender-hairted, and he cudn't bear t' come home to all dat sorrer an' trouble, and he jest natchelly lit right out wid dem same darkies fo' de cotton boat. But fust he done sole his mule, an' dat how come I got wu'd from him. I ben nigh deestractid, sarchin' fo' him far an' near!"

"You poor thing! what did you do?" said Dorothy, in a gentle voice, at the sound of which the muscles about the black woman's mouth twitched a little.

"T'ank ye, ma'am," she said; "yes, ma'am, I p'intedly did have a rough time, dat fall.   De jedge got so mad at Jake usin' of him dat mean, not knowin' how chicken-hairtid Jake ben, an' how he jest cudn't bear nohow to see folkses suffer—so de jedge, not knowin', wudn't holp me; an' de man wid de morgige, he come down on me de 'p'inted time, an' looked like I hadn't no ways to turn. But I did reason wid dat man, an' I got him to take a new morgige 'stiddier dat ole one, if I wud pay fo' hunderd dolla's 'stiddier two hunderd an' fo'ty; an' den he let me off, an' I did stay right along at my own place, a-waitin' on Jake, 'cause I knowed he wud come back some day.   And I got a mighty good crap nex' year, an' I made out wid de pickin' an' de stock; an' so I paid off most de morgige an' all er de jedge's money. I ben sho' all 'long dat Jake be comin' back; an' one day, 'long 'bout sundown, I seen a cullud man a-comin' down de lane mighty slow and tuckered-out like. Dat ar ben Jake. He suttinly did look distressid, w'arin' de ve'y selfsame clo'es he done got on his back when he lit out, an' kinder puny-lookin' an' coughin' like he got de breas' complaint. He says: 'Doesn't ye know me, Persis?' Den he cudn't speak fo' de coughin'; and me, I——"

She stopped with a gulp; so unlike the ordinary African fashion of manifesting emotion was her subdued self-restraint, that it took the Lawrences a moment to realize that she was overcome by the recollection of the meeting.

"I suttinly did feel good, dat time, to git Jake back. I got him inter de house, an' got a cup of coffee down him, an' kinder spi'ted him up; so den he tole me how he ben in Memphis, dat great city, an' had a turrible hard time, an' he seen a man—dat ben Unk' Jerusalem Coffin—come from we-all's way, an' he axed him to lend him some change, 'cause he didn't know whar to turn fo' a bite er bread or a bite er po'k—he got down so bad like dat! And Unk' Jerusalem, he bu'st out laffin' an' tole him it ben right funny fo' a man ownin' a good farm to be gwine hungry dat-a-way! An' wid dat, Jake got excited an' axed him questins an' borried what he cud, an' come right spang home by de nex' boat. Well, ayfter dat, we-all paid de res' er de morgige an' got 'long right good, an' sent de boy—dat ben Jake's boy, ye know, sah——"

"He was a widower, then, when you married him?"

"Yes, sah; suttinly, sah. Jake's fust wife ben Sist' Viney Griffin; belong to we-all's chu'ch, a right good woman, dat made de bes' kind er light bread. She died up an' lef' Jake wid de baby, de onlies' chile dey got, him risin' of two. Looked like dey didn't have nobuddy to do fo' dem, so I jes' taken de chile to my own place. I ben doin' well, an' dey ben mighty po'. Dat how come I taken up wid Jake in de fust place; I got sorter wonted to doin' fo' him, 'cause he 'd be comin' to see de baby, an' I wud men' him up—him havin' nobuddy. An' we did get 'long right well tell dat 'ar Lize Ma'y, she sot 'er eyes on my Jake an' made her brags she ben gwine t' marry him afo' nex' Christmas. An' she kep' up a-laffin' an' a-laffin'; an' ever' festival Jake done go ter, dar ben dat Lize Ma'y a-laffin' at him! Dat made him kinder curi's an' cravin' fo' to know what fo' she keep up dat laffin'; men pussons is dat way—dey sots deir min's on mo' fool t'ings dan de women; I had de crap to look ayfter, an' de keerin' fo' de stock an' de cookin', an' a power er t'ings to keep me busy. 'Sides, I cudn't leave de chile by his lone, to go to festivals; but I cudn't enjure to 'prive Jake er takin' his time an' his pleasure. So he did go, an' he met up wid her ever' time; an' bymeby he got to axin' of her 'bout de laffin', an' bymeby agin she didn't laff no mo', an' dat how come all de trouble. One day, he lef' me in the mo'nin', makin' out like he ben gwine to take a load er wood to de jedge; an' I ain't seen him tell dis day.

But a man come an' showed me a paper dat he sayed ben sign by me; an' dat like 'nuff, seein' Jake got me to sign my name to whut he did call jest a lettin' him sell de bit of wood. An' he say, dat man, dat I done sign 'way de hull plum' place, an' dat Jake got de money——"

Husband and wife exchanged glances, both recalling that Jake had come to the Black river with a most surprising plenitude of ready money.

"Well, sah," she continued, "I wen' to de jedge; but he did say as how I done sign de paper, an' de place ben Jake's fo' to sell, an' I cudn't do nuffin'. An' I went to ax him to cotch Jake fo' me, an' git him back; but he sayed dat he cudn't fin' him. An' den I sole de truck an' de stock, an' pack up what I cudn't sell, an' come a-sarchin' fo' Jake; 'cause I knowed 't didn't ben no good waitin' on him, 'cause dar didn't ben nuffin' fo' him to come back ter! I ben trackin' him ever since; but I got him now, sho'."

She smiled; the inscrutable part of the whole business was that she should be so confident that it would be concluded in her favor, if once she were face to face with the fugitives.

"I 'lows," she said, "Jake done fool away a heap er dat money; but he kain't of got shet er it all.   We kin make mo'—— "

Here she stopped and stared down the winding road from the forest.

Along the sun-dappled roadway, rattling and jingling, came a smart new wagon, drawn by two young horses of mettle enough to toss their heads and shy at pools of water here and there.   The front seat of the wagon was filled by the voluminous white draperies of the only occupant, a handsome yellow girl, whose eyes rolled under an astonishing flower pot of a hat, and whose white gown was decked with a motley flutter of ribbons.   She glittered with plated jewelry and red and green and yellow glass and Arkansas diamonds.

Pompously she held herself erect, and tossed her ringleted head at the gaping crowd of darkies.

"Heabenly name! dat sho' de colts," muttered the wife; "look a' de way dat fool nigger dribe—wabble f'om one side er de road to de udder, like a goose a-runnin'. Lize Ma'y, I done come fo' Jake."

The splendidly attired one stopped and looked at the old wife standing in the dusty road in her homely gown.

At first, she winced; but in a second, recovering herself, she tossed her head in vast scorn.

"Go 'long, nigger, then," she said, distinctly; "you wicked woman, ain't you 'shamed to come runnin' ayfter my husband? You' a heap too old to be actin' so scandilous!"

Persis only gasped, "You' husband?" and stared at her as a fish stares, jerked out into the maddening air.

Some intention that Lize Ma'y had of stopping at the store she must have quickly abandoned, for she lashed the horses.

"Stop!" thundered Lawrence; not that he was excited, but to be heard above her wheels and the laughter of the idlers.

She made as if she did not hear; but he waved his arm at her, and she had not the audacity to sail past him, the white man.

Sullenly she drew in her horses; but then, as if by the switching away of a curtain, her face was revealed, all coy smiles, and she said:

"Was you seekin' anything, sah?"

"Yes; I have something to say to you. Why did you inveigle that poor woman's husband away from her?"

"Laws, sah, she does be po' an' old, but that ain't my fault; I kain't holp 'er bein' born so long befo' me—that ben the Lord's will an' not mine. An' I does hate to say it 'bout 'er, but she is the one takin' away husban's, for she is aimin' to take away mine. She never was Jake's wife—no, sah, never; an' when he met up with me, he got 'shamed of himself, an' he lef' his wickedness an' married me. An' then she threatened his life, an' so we come 'way down here."

This was said with a touching mien of modesty that had like to have impressed the man who listened, but his wife laughed.

"Do you mean to say you are Jake's wife, and not this one?"

"Yes, sah—yes'm. I ben married by

Squire Nixon, an' I got de writings correct. Ax 'er who married 'er to Jake."

"It ben a minister, an' he is daid!" said Persis, frowning.

"But you is sho' got some writings 'bout it, to show?" said Lize Ma'y, insolently gentle.

"You knows I ain't; you knows Jake stole de stockin' wid de money whar dey ben!" said Persis, between her teeth, still staring in the same daze.

"I like for to go to my husband, if you please, sah," said Lize Ma'y, with much suavity; "I ain't 'customed t' be holdin' talk with sich pussons. I don't aim to give 'er no bad talk, but I ask 'er jest to leave us 'lone an' quit interferin' with married folks. 'Tain't decent."

She inclined her bedecked head to the colonel and his wife, and was for making off again. Again the colonel stopped her.

"Hold a minute!" said he — his wife had whispered in his ear; "I want to hear what Jake has to say for himself, before you talk it over together. Hi! you Jim, run up and tell Jake to come over here!"

There was a pause that the discarded wife filled up by going over to the little boy. She was visibly agitated. "You' daddy a-comin', Jakey," she said. "Is you got you' face clean? Make haste an' git you' new cap on!"

The erring Jake, when he appeared, escorted by no less than six interested black brethren, showed a mild, rather attractive yellow face and a smart new suit of clothes of the gay plaids that lie in heaps on the counters of "all-sort stores" in the south. A flimsy red silk handkerchief stood in a triangle out of one pocket. He drew it forth, wiped his face and grinned feebly, first at one claimant and then at the other.

"I done come fo' ye, Jake," said Persis, in a quiet way.

Lize Ma'y writhed her shapely head and shrugged her shoulders, giggling:

"Cunnel is cravin' to know if you is my husban' or hers, Jake."

Before Jake answered, he hopped nimbly into the wagon. Then he said:

"I reckon I belongs to Lize Ma'y."

"But this woman here says you married

her first," objected the colonel; "hold those horses still, will you, Jake?"

"Does be powerful skeery and restive," muttered Jake, while he drew in the reins with a wide crooking of his elbows and loud "Huh! quit you' funnin'!" and hissing sounds between his teeth.

"I nev' did marry her 'tall," said he, "nev' in this worl'; jes' ta'en up wid her, an' dat 's all—ain't it, Lize Ma'y?"

"Dat 's a lie!" said Persis.

"Who knows that you were married up in Tennessee?" Dorothy struck in.

To her surprise, Persis's face fell.

"I done tole de judge dat, an' he sayed whar did I ben mah'ied, 'cause it ben afo' we-uns did move to Tennessee; an' he sayed did I got are writin's, an' I didn't, 'cause Jake stole dem; an' he sayed I cudn't prove it.   But I don't guess Jake wud t'ar up dem papers dat we allus did keep so keerful."

Lize Ma'y's muttered chorus of scorn rose into a groan:

"Oh, jes' hark to the lies of her!   She knows there ain't no papers!"

"I am sorry," said the colonel; "but, if

you have no proof of the marriage, I really can't interfere, under the circumstances."

"T'ank you, sir," said Lize Ma'y; "but one t'ing mo': Jake an' me, we is right willin' to take little Jakey home an' keer fo' him."

"Yes, sah—suttinly, sah; we is, fo' a fac'!" Jake agreed, eagerly, with a look at the boy. "Come on by, Jakey; ain't ye gwine speak to dad?"

But Jakey, though he grinned responsively, held back, saying:

"Mummer, too?"

For the first time, Jake looked uncomfortable; he stole a glance at the ugly sad face of the woman standing in the dust, and then winced at some unseen prod from the girl by his side and tried to pass it off with a laugh.

"Come on," said Lize Ma'y, "the chile belongs to you; she cayn't claim him."

"I don't like for to toll him 'way from 'er," muttered Jake; "but if ye want to git shet er him, Persis, I are right willin'——"

The woman's face quivered a little.

"No," said she, quietly, "I don't." At

the same time, she suddenly flung both her arms about the small body pressed among her skirts, and glared at Lize Ma'y, who smiled back.

"You ain't got nothin' to say 'bout it," was the taunt in which Lize Ma'y expressed both hate and triumph; "he ain't no kin to you!"

Mrs. Lawrence came to the rescue of her perplexed husband with a calm feminine disregard of the visible claims of the law of the land.

"Jake, you go right home," she said; "you both ought to be ashamed of yourselves. We are going to find out about this. You can come back to-morrow."

Lize Ma'y would have spoken, but for her companion; he read the light in Dorothy's eye too shrewdly for resistance. Without a word, he hit the horses a swinging clip with the twig that served as whip, and the wagon whirled off in a cloud of dust.

Only Dorothy noted the tears slowly gather in the deserted wife's eyes. Not a word did she speak. She made a rude kind of courtesy to the white lady, and, with the child still clinging to her skirts, she moved away.   They saw her climb into the wagon.

"Well, I am sorry for her," said Dorothy; "I think she was his wife."

"There is no telling," said the colonel, philosophically; "I reckon she can't do anything if she is."

"Can't she go to law?"

"She couldn't prove anything if she did."

"Well, I don't think much of the law, then!" cried Dorothy, with true feminine logic, according to the masculine notion of it.

The colonel dismissed the matter from his mind.   Dorothy was less easily swayed when her sympathies were moved.

"I wonder if she can wash," she mused aloud, in the morning.

"There, I nearly cut myself," said the colonel, who was shaving himself, and thus easily ruffled.   "Who can wash?"

"Why, Persis, of course—Jake's wife. We might have her do our extra washing this week, and then she could stay on and have a chance to win back Jake."

"She is more likely to lose the child—

Lize Ma'y means business; and she has no legal claim."

"Isn't there any court she could go to?"

"Well, hardly."

"I think it a very great shame, Phil; and I am going to talk to that Jake."

Mrs. Lawrence was in earnest. The colonel laughed, but he drove her to Jake's in the cool of the morning, just the same.

They were both surprised to find, in front of the house, a white-covered mover's wagon; and their surprise deepened and thrilled into amaze when a tall woman put her head out of the door. The woman was Persis. At the same moment, Jake's slim figure and gentle smile drifted into view from around the wood pile.

He smiled sheepishly at the colonel's salutation.

"Oh, yes, sir," said he; "dat Persis fo' sho', boss! "You see," he rubbed his hands softly together, "she come by right early, befo' sun-up, 'most. I ben kinder upset by dat 'ar Lize Ma'y, onyhow, an' I ben studyin' 'bout t'ings. Den up comes Persis an' gits out befo' you cud bat you' eye, and is gwine

in de house, an' all she says ben: 'I done
come fo' my Jake,' says she; an' dat 'ar fool
yaller gell, she ben fixin' to laff an' laff.
Persis, she nev' did git mad—jes' says: 'I
ben to de cunnel, an' I ben to de jedge, an'
no redressance nur holp, an' I taken it inter
my own han's, Lize Ma'y,' says she; an'
'clare if dat triflin' Lize Ma'y didn't bu'st
out laffin' so ye cud hear 'er clear an' across
de creek. An' den Persis, she nev' did
pyart lips wid 'er no more—jes' falled on
'er an' pulled out a big pawpaw switch an'
guv 'er de bud most outrigeous. Yes, sah,
she did lick dat gell twell she squealed an'
hollered an' run outen de house, an' den she
made me run fotch all 'er clo'es an' fling
dem ayfter 'er."

"But didn't you interfere?" said the colonel, with a strong desire to laugh.

Jake rolled his mild eyes.

"I don't reckon you ev' did see Persis
excited," answered he, solemnly; "Persis, she don' sull nor she don' r'ar on ye,
but she's terrible hefty in her arms! No,
sah; I doesn't 'low to bunch rags wid dat
nigger, if I kin holp it!"

"But you were mighty easy with her yesterday!"

"Den I ben in de wagon, sah; dat 'ar does make a heap o' differ."

"What did you do?"

"Why, I stan's mighty still an' reasons wid Persis, an' begs 'er not to hu't Lize Ma'y too hyard; and den I goes in, an' Persis done make me some er de bestis coffee an' corn bread."

At this moment, Persis put her head out of the door, and both man and woman grinned.

"Well, you got him back, didn't you?" said Dorothy.

"In co'se," Persis replied; "I knowed I cud git Jake back, if I jest got a little place to argy wid him in!"

"I was mistaken," the colonel explained to his wife; "there was still a resource, and Persis appealed to the court of last resort."

Why Abbylonia Surrendered

Why Abbylonia Surrendered.

Love that hath us in his net,
Shall he pass and we forget?
*   *   *   *   *   *   *

Love is hurt by jar and fret,
Love becomes a vague regret,
Eyes with idle tears are wet,
Idle habit links us yet.
What is love, for we forget!
Ah no! no!   —*Tennyson.*

ABBYLONIA EDDINGS, wife to the Reverend Eli Eddings, was always tired of a Monday afternoon; but never had she been so exhausted, soul and body, as she was one Monday in March. She stood in a tired woman's attitude, her knuckles on her hips, and gazed wearily about the kitchen. "Just slicked up!" sighed Abbylonia. "Well, it's the best I can do, with *this* back."

Yet the ordinary eye would have reported the room miraculously neat, from the big dresser to the glistening kitchen stove. But the eye of Abbylonia Eddings was no ordinary eye. She had more ambition than health, and in spite of eking out the latter with that which the New Englanders name "faculty," and we in Arkansas call by no special name, but admire as sincerely, she at times strained her nerves to the tearing point.

"Abby," her mother-in-law, the widow Eddings, once said to her — "Abby, you had ought to *pray* to be more trifling!"

"I 'll die sooner," replied Abby, vehemently. "Do you want me to sink to the level of these people around me? I can work, whether I 'm tired or rested. There wouldn't be much done if I only worked when I was rested."

"But you 're working on your *nerves*, Abby," the widow ventured, "and they won't last forever."

"I reckon they 'll last *my* time," said Abby.

The widow shook her head and wiped

away an unobtrusive tear. She was a
woman of a gentle and plaintive turn, who
said , little, but wept frequently and at
length. Abby herself seldom wept. Perhaps it were better for her had she thus
washed the bitterness out of her heart.
She did not shed any tears to-day, although
she was crushed under the leaden misery
of her anxieties and her physical exhaus-
tion. She looked, dry-eyed, out of the window — not to see the street, but simply
because the window happened to be in front
of her eyes — and caught a glimpse of her
mother-in-law's black mohair skirts brush-
ing past her gate. "There comes maw,"
she said, "because I don't feel like seeing a
mortal creature! Well, I don't care. I'd
like maw to remember me kindly." The
last thought summoned a flicker of a smile
to her face as she opened the door.

The widow Eddings lived down the
street, in her own house, which her son
Eli had bought for her. He had selected
this little village because Hattie, Mrs. Eddings's daughter, lived there, being married
to one of the best tempered and most un-

successful business men in the state of Arkansas. Eli had loaned him money twice (although Abby knew it would be lost), and now had hit upon the expedient of yoking him to a shrewd partner, who should manage the business, while Bud Slater might entertain the customers.

The widow came in gingerly, on tip-toe. "Dreadful muddy," said she; "and I 'lowed 'twas only shoe-mouth deep, and come off without my rubbers. I had to come most of the crossing on the railroad; and I was scared to death lest a train should come up behind, kinder quiet like, whilst I ben so busy picking my way, and run over me ——"

"I don't think there 's much danger of a train of cyars being *quiet*, maw," said Abby, who was wiping off the widow's shoes.

"Well, they do make a heap of noise in the street. But I didn't aim to contrairy you, Abby; I reckon you know best, reading so many books as *you* do." The widow sighed. She had a long, fair, plaintive face and timid eyes. There was a scar over one eyebrow. She was always carefully neat in her dress, which was black, not so much because she still mourned the husband of her youth (who used to throw things at her) as because she esteemed black an economical and useful habit. She continued: "There 's a dreadful sight of typhoid fever in town. I reckon it 's the mud puddles. Do you know you got a reg'lar slash outside the gate? I seen Susy Nell playing outside; she looked kinder puny, I 'lowed. Maybe not."

Susy Nell was the Eddings's only child. Abby could have explained her looks, but she had no mind for talk. The widow dismally continued to unpack her budget: "Say, Abby — I reckon I best tell you, for you 're sure to hear it — Eli ain't going to git the job of painting the church pews."

"They didn't give it to Hobson?"

"That 's jest what they did. I met Mis' Hobson on the street, and she told me herself. Right spiteful of her, too, I call it. But 'tain't right to jedge. Jedge not, and you ain't going to be jedged, you know. She was with Sister Arnott."

"That 's how Hobson got the job," said

Abby. But she showed none of that in-
dignation that the widow had expected.
"She's always toadying Mrs. Arnott. And
anything Brother Arnott says, you know
——"

"Yes, the committee 'll jest grease its
head and swaller it whole," said the widow,
sadly. "I expect she talked him over.
What do you think she had in her hand,
Abby?"

"I don't know, maw." Abby spoke list-
lessly.

"It was that dress pattern you told me
you aimed to buy."

"The blue mixture with the red thread
in it?"

"Yes, ma'am. That very piece. It was
sticking out of the bundle. And I felt so
bad 'bout you being disappointed of that
dress that I went round to the store, thinking maybe Bud might have some come in
or something, and that's how come they
sold it, and thinkin' I'd git it for you, to
make sure——"

"Maw, that was right sweet and kind of
you," exclaimed Abby; her heart smote her

with the remembrance of many kindnesses from her dismal mother-in-law, dolefully rendered, but in all willingness of heart.

"I don't guess you need to be thankful, Abby; didn't come to nothing. I only found out that they didn't have nare 'nother bit. Bud had spoken to Mis' Arnott how you thought of taking the piece; but he said that only seemed to make her more wishful to have it, and he didn't like to mad her, she buys so much."

"Sister Arnott has been mean to us all ever since we came," said Abby; but, to the widow's surprise, she said it without violence. There was an absent look in her eye, dissipated for a second by the petty sting of the news, but returning at once. "I reckon the Arnotts would be glad to have us quit. Brother Arnott's got a nephew he thinks Elder would assign here."

"Oh laws, Abby! But he cayn't!" cried the widow, in dismay.

"Not unless Eli's willing; but — maw, Eli wants to leave the ministry!"

"Well, *sir!*" the widow gasped. She was not able to say more; her lips moved

up and down like the gills of a fish out of
water.

"It isn't like it was a question of sup-
port." Abby spoke doggedly. "Eli earns
far more by his painting and papering than
he does at preaching. You know what little
places we 've been at — making a crop and
Eli preaching round. Yet we 've laid by
some money. I 've slaved night and day,
hoping we could leave the country and come
to some civilized place. Eli 's been away
most of the time papering and painting,
coming back to the circuit to preach Sundays. The conference made no objections,
because he always did his full duty, and he
was willing to take such little pay. It was
lonesome for me, but I was willing to bear
it, always hoping he would get a better circuit. And I was *so* happy when we moved
here. But now Eli says he must quit. He
has enough to buy a little farm if he cayn't
open a shop here — maw, don't cry like
that!"

The widow had taken out her handkerchief, and quietly, but in a thorough-going
manner, with no attempt to gainstrive it,

was abandoning herself to grief. Her first words were, "Reckon I got to ask you to give me another han'kercher, Abbylonia; I set out not knowing I 'd have occasion to use it, excepting for ordinary purposes, and I picked up little Hattie's, and it 's so small that I — I got to trouble you!"

She mopped her eyes patiently with the small cotton square until the fresh handkerchief appeared, when the deferred flood swept over the barriers of control and she wept aloud.

"Oh, he was a child of prayer!" — so articulate speech shaped itself in the chaos of woeful sounds. "When he wasn't more 'n twelve year old I told him I wanted him to be a preacher, and I begun reading of him sermons on a Sunday — and — he never *did* like 'em! He always wanted to paint and to chop things with the hatchet. He painted the hull wood shed different colors, to see how they 'd look; and I used to pray over him and cry nights. I don't guess buckets on buckets would hole my tears; and at last you come to visit in the neighborhood, and he begun to wait on you, and you persuaded of him — oh, Lordy! how kin I bear it if he gives it up now! And this a heap the best place he ever did git!"

"The only decent place," said Abby.

"How come it, Abby? You taking in sech a heap of books and papers, they ain't led Eli astray, have they? That magazine on the table, are you sure it's sound religiously? The kiver is plumb worldly, to my mind. He ain't lost his faith?"

"He hates to preach, and he loves to paint. I reckon that's it, as near as I can ascertain."

The widow rocked to and fro, sobbing. There were no tears in Abby's eyes; her mouth was rigid.

"If he wasn't so obstinate," mourned the widow. "He always did be mule-headed, even as a little boy. . He was mild as milk, but once get him to make up his mind, and there wasn't nare moving of him."

"We did move him once," said Abby; "he didn't ever want to be a minister."

"But look how well he's done — look at his sermons ——" Her speech snapped off short; and both women colored. "Oh,

Abby, I cayn't keep it from you no longer;
I 've known it all along!" the widow cried.

Abby smiled bitterly. "Well, maw, I
reckon I 'm glad. And you never told——"

"I never told a mortal soul. Not Hattie;
not nobody."

"I 'm sure you didn't, maw, or Bud would
have had it all over town."

"Abby, is it *that?*"

"Yes, maw, it 's that. He says he can't
endure it any longer."

"I 'low you 've always done it."

"Always. He never wrote a word himself. I wrote them, and he learned them,
sometimes. More times he 's read them
off."

"It has been right hard on you, Abby."

Abby turned away her head; then she
flung it back, and her eyes were glowing.
"Yes, it has been hard, maw; but it 's been
a comfort in a way, too. You know how I
always have hungered after books and
papers. Maw, every cent of Eli's salary
he 's given me. He *would* do it. He 's
made a good living for us beside. And I 've
bought magazines and papers and books. I

like having the money. But I liked the ——
I don't know whether you 'll understand
me, but there 's something in me that had
to come out, and it came out in the sermons;
and when I got so unhappy it was a strange
kind of comfort to talk about troubles that
were not like mine, yet, being troubles,
made a suffering that *was* like mine."

"They always were powerful good sermons, Abby. But what were you unhappy
about, daughter? Losing of the baby, of
course, but anything else? Has this here
you doing his work made a differ between
you two?"

"Something has," said Abby; "he — he's
kind as ever, but he tells me nothing. I
know he 's miserable. I 've known it a long
time, but he never has said a word until last
week. Then, all at once, he told me he
couldn't endure it any longer; he felt he
was a fraud. As long as he was working
round at little places, doing more pastoral
work than preaching, it hadn't seemed so
bad to him. I asked him what he was going
to say, and he said, 'The truth!' He was

going to get up in church and make confession before God and man ——— "

"Oh, laws, Abby, you mustn't let him do *that!*" cried the widow.

"I don't know if I can help it," said Abby, with a kind of groan. "Oh, maw, you don't understand." She bit her lips; even to her husband's mother the wife could not say: "You don't understand how little influence I have over him."

"Yes, I do, tew, Abby; he's powerful obstinate. And I reckon it's hard for a man to feel his wife's smarter 'n him!"

"I'm not, and I don't think it," said Abby; "but maw, you never told me — how did you find out?"

"Oh, easy," sighed the widow; "the sermons was like you and not like Eli, and one night I found some sheets of paper in the wood box. I couldn't help finding out — laws, Abby, there's Eli himself!"

"Abby! Is Abby here?" said a deep, mild voice. "Why, maw, is it you? Rest your bonnet on a chair and stay to supper with us."

Eli had opened the door and was before

them, a tall figure, stooping a little, with a handsome face. The curly brown hair was wearing away on the temples. They were well shaped temples, and the forehead was a promising dome. The features beneath, too, were clear cut and manly, and the eyes were bright, but the whole countenance wore a deprecating expression that made one think of a dog expecting a blow, and for which there was no sufficient reason either in Eli Eddings's nature or prospects. He was a Methodist minister, who was known favorably among the brethren as one who asked for little from the conference, went willingly to the least desirable circuits, and preached impassioned sermons in an apathetic manner.

The widow kissed her son tearfully, but she could not be persuaded to stay, and he followed her voyage through the mud puddles with an anxious eye.

"Ain't maw been crying?" said he.

"You 're right observing, Eli," said Abby, dryly. "Yes, she has."

"I hope it wasn't anything serious, Abby."

"That's as you look at it, Eli. She was crying about your leaving the ministry."

"I was 'fraid she would take it that way," said Eli. And he sighed.

"I don't know when I've seen your mother so worked up, Eli; it's going to be a most terrible thing to her if you do the way you said."

Eli's lips puckered with pain. He said nothing, and his silence and the very misery of his bearing pricked his wife's temper. She was exasperated and frightened at once. The thought darted to her, "He's fixing not to give in, no matter how it hurts him!" Her anger flashed out before she could ask herself was it wise to speak. "It's a cruel, unmanly thing you propose to do, Eli Eddings," she cried — "shaming your mother and me before all these strangers. You may have a right to confess your own sins, if you will call them that, but you've no right to confess *mine!*"

"But, Abby" — Eli found his voice — "you didn't do wrong; it was *me*. All the same, if you don't want it, I can jest say I didn't write the sermons. I won't speak your name."

Abby shivered. "I think," said she, slowly, in an emotionless voice, "that if you lived with me a hundred years you wouldn't understand me, Eli."

"Maybe not," Eli answered, patiently. "I expect I had better pack up some water for you, Abby, and fill the wood box." Therewith he was edging out of the room.

"Can't you see the box is full?" said Abby. "Johnny Hinds filled it. He was over here. Susy Nell fell in the cistern —— " The father's face changed sharply before she could add, "Of course I pulled her out; I heard the splash and there she was, floundering —— "

"And it's eight feet deep, and you cayn't swim! Oh Lord, Abby, what did you do?"

"Threw the clothes line to her, of course, and told her to catch on and hold on or I'd whip her! What else could I do? She'd have drowned before I could rummage up that ladder in the barn!"

"But how did you pull her up?"

"I called on Johnny Hinds, who was out

in their yard, and *he* ran over. I made him get that long board you had for papering, and I had him put it down crossways in the cistern, and I hauled her to the board, and she climbed out enough for me to catch her."

"You — you weren't mad at her, Abby?" Eli spoke timidly, and Abbylonia's eyes turned to steel.

"Didn't I tell you she caught on to the rope as I told her? Do you suppose I 'd punish her for minding of me? No; I boiled her some milk and gave Johnny and her some doughnuts. I had to change every stitch on her."

Eddings swallowed twice. "You 're awful smart, Abby!" said he. Then he cleared his throat; but nothing came of the exercise, and presently he shuffled out of the room.

Abbylonia sank into a chair, leaned her head back, and laughed. "That 's all the good it 's done, my telling," she said to herself; "he 's gone to hug and kiss *her;* he hasn't a thought left for *me.* He didn't even kiss me once. What do I care? When he does, it 's only because he promised to love his wife. It 's his duty. Well, I don't blame him. I 'm ugly tempered and I 'm homely; I 'm worn to the bone working for him. Oh, Lord! Oh, Lord! How can you make a woman like me, who can't make her husband love her, and can't stop loving him!" She walked to the little glass above the roller towel and gazed steadily on her image. The sunlight gave her every wrinkle. Mercilessly it painted the irregular sharp features, the straight black hair, the unquiet eyes, the lines scoring the brow between the eyebrows (like footprints of a frown), the set mouth, the crooked curve of the jaw. The attractions of the face, its clear soft tints, the brilliancy of the eyes, and the white teeth that showed in a flashing smile, the refinement of those irregular features, the vitality and changing intensity that informed the whole plain countenance — these, which were poor Abby's real charm, she could not see, and the picture was gallsome to her. She turned away with a groan. "He 's a good man," she thought, "but nobody can be so cruel as good people. To get rest for his own conscience he 's willing to send me to perdition! I 'll die before I 'll go back and live on a farm again, with Eli away half the time. And I wouldn't even have the sermons to write and the little money for my own." How much comfort she found in the spending of that pittance, without let or hindrance, on the books for which she hungered, is beyond the imagination of one who has not been a dependent step-daughter, filching a crude education from sleep, and picking cotton to earn the price of a print gown. "Yes," she repeated, "I 'll die sooner!" Under all her physical and mental torture, even while she called herself hopeless, she had been hoping that Eli would be moved by the danger to the child and by her rescue, and that she could use his awakened tenderness to soften his purpose. The hope had failed.

"I 'll give him *one* last chance," she said. "I 'll not be angry or bitter. I 'll speak to him calmly and kindly. We 'll talk it over, and at least he 'll not be so cruel as to speak out; he can quit the ministry without making the town too hot to hold us."

Trying to blow the dead embers of her hope into life after this fashion, she went about preparing a better supper than usual for Eli.   She was so footsore that every step hurt her, and there were shooting pains in her back, but she moved briskly. Whatever Abby lacked, it was not fortitude. Eli came in, laden with wood, and Susy Nell at his heels carried a basket of kindling.

"Susy Nell's been giving Johnny a beautiful knife," said Eli, in a cheerful high tone, "and papa's going to paint Johnny's mamma's parlor for her to-morrow — to show how good we think he was to pull Susy Nell out of the mean, bad cistern.   Now Susy 's going to be mamma's little helpin' dirl, ain't she?"

Susy Nell, a chubby, smiling little creature of five, proffered the basket, and Abby kissed her, saying, "Now you run out and play."   Susy Nell felt vaguely repulsed, but she took it in good part, and pattered away for the yard.   She forgot the kisses which (as agreed outside) she was to give "dear mamma for pulling her out of the cistern." And Eli was too after-witted to remind her. He busied himself making the fire and cutting the meat.

"Maw told me you didn't get the painting of the pews."

Eli avoided her eye. "No, Abby; they gave it to Hobson. Maybe I hadn't ought to say it, but I 'm afraid they 'll make a botch of it, too. They don't understand fine work."

"They certainly don't," said Abby; "they painted Hattie's aunt's house, and the paint streaked dark streaks the very next summer."

"Put turpentine in it, and most likely used boiled linseed oil," said Eli, with a sudden air of interest. "Well, I would hate to have them spoil those pews. I wonder would they take it hard if I was to caution them against boiled oil, and ask 'em to put plenty of japan in the paint for the inside. They 're going to varnish the pews, they say; and if they ain't careful and don't use the right kind of hard finish, which takes a heap of rubbing and goes on

mighty slow like, there 'll be trouble for
sure."

"But why did Brother Arnott not get *you*
to do it? you the minister, too, and having
an interest —— "

"Well, he said that was the very reason
— said ministers of the Gospel had no right
to be engaged in secular callings. I reckon
he 's partly right, too."

"Are you of the same mind still, Eli?"

"If I 'd thought of changing, how *could* I
ayfter the Lord's dealing with me this
day?"

"Do you think the Lord pulled her out of
the cistern? or maybe you think He pushed
her *in*," said Abby. She had turned around.
Her face was flushed, and her eyes glittered, and she spoke in an unfamiliar voice.

Eli's sluggish wits could not rally under
her vehemence. "I — I reckon we better
not talk about it till you feel cammer,
Abby," he stammered. Which was about
the most irritating thing that he could have
said.

Abby had begun the interview determined not to grow angry; but poor Abby,

with her raw nerves and the canker-fret of jealousy in her heart, was not in a condition to discuss the merits of baking powder, safely. The passion that she had tried to smother, blazed up at Eli's words. She flung out her arms wildly, crying: "It's now or never, Eli Eddings. For the last time, and mighty near the first time too, I'm going to ask you to consider *me*. It is folly of you to imagine we can live on here ayfter your getting up and making that confession. I couldn't show my face among the ladies here. *I* have a little sense of shame, if you haven't!"

Eli hung his head. "We could go into the country and rent and make a crop ——"

"I *hate* the country! I hate the country people!"

"You didn't hate the folks at Sycamore Hurd when they were so kind to us, when little Eli died, and put up a stone to his grave, and Sister Mitchell picked all the geraniums she was saving for Rosy's wedding — you don't hate *them*, Abby?" said Eli, sorrowfully. And his patience, instead of quelling Abby's wrath, only made it mount the higher; it seemed to put her in the wrong, who was really in the right.

Except for the goading of her fury she could never have answered him so cruelly; but nothing seems cruel to an angry wife who has disputed with her husband. She said: "If we hadn't been out in Sycamore Hurd, if you 'd taken the other circuit they offered, and been in town near a doctor, perhaps baby wouldn't have died!"

Eli recoiled, and his face went white. Abby was not looking at him; she had whisked back to her frying pan on the stove; when the hot grease spattered on her wrist she smiled savagely at the pain. Her husband's voice came after a long pause:

"I don't guess there 's much use our talking, Abby; if there ain't anything I can do to help you 'bout supper I reckon I 'll go out in the yard with Susy Nell."

"Eli, are you going to speak out next Sunday?"

"We won't talk 'bout it now, Abby. You —you pray, too, and then we 'll talk."

"Eli, no prayer will change this to me.

And I tell you now, you 'll be sorrier than you ever were in your life if you do speak."

Eli made no reply at all. He left the house. He carried away a deep wound of his own; and pain always made him silent. But again his silence infuriated his wife. At supper she told him that Susy Nell was coughing, and she had best stay with her that night.

"Don't you think we 'd ought to have the doctor step in?" said Eli, anxiously, "Is your throat sore, honey lamb?"

He made no slightest objection. Abby staid with Susy Nell every night that week. The cold had disappeared — if there ever had been a cold — but Eli did not speak of a change.

"He 's glad to be rid of me," thought the miserable wife; "all he cares for is Susy Nell," and her anger changed into something deadly and still. At times she was conscious that her torment of soul was overmuch for anything that Eli had done. Then she would tell herself that she had lost her husband's love, and she would have to grow old and haggard in the slavery of a farm, and gradually, as her health failed, that she would sink into the like of the slatternly drudges that she despised. She felt her strength failing. She could not do half the work that she used to do unless she lashed herself through the last part of her tasks. Years of overtaxed days and robbed nights were having their revenge. The creeping paralysis of estrangement had aided them, and the shock of Eli's decision dealt the last blow. Abby's nervous system simply collapsed. She did not suspect it, but she was not a responsible creature.

There was a strange sensation in her head all the time. It seemed to her that she was conscious of the physical working of her thoughts, and that as they passed from one chamber of her brain to another, she felt the passage. Once this notion had fastened on her mind, she could not pluck it away, and the wearisome disquietude of it, it is impossible to suggest. Unreal noises began to vex her ears. She would hear her dead baby cry; wailing voices would rise and sink, which, no sooner did she hearken, would cease or change into the clamor of the poultry yard. At first the ghastly path of escape from her trouble had been only the mental elaboration of her angry phrase, "I 'll die sooner!"

Then she did not mean to die; but inch by inch the tide of despair submerged the nervous woman's reason. The fancy became a possibility; at last it was a desire.

"I 'm growing crazy, I expect." said Abby. "Well, it don't matter, if I can die in time!"

It may be asked, had Abby no religious scruples regarding the sin that she meditated? Not any. It is the besetting temptation of the handler of religious things to lose his reverence in the familiarity of habit. Every clergyman knows the deadening effect of the constant use of religious phraseology. And Abby had no protection of religious zeal. She was not a pious woman. She wrote her sermons not to save souls, but to help the Reverend Eli Eddings. From indifference she had slipped into doubt.

"If there is a God, He knows I cayn't bear it!" she said.

Thus it came to pass that she no longer watched Eli's face for signs of relenting. She withdrew into the shadow of her distempered dreams.   Here was a way to punish Eli, all the dearer because it would make her suffer as well as him.   A woman always likes to strike the man that she loves through her own heart.

So the soul of Eli's wife walked apart among formless hopes and fears, or beat against that *impasse*, a realization of the next step beyond the gate.   Yet to outward seeming she was not changed, except that she was a trifle absent minded.   Until Friday she had a faint — was it hope or fear? —that Eli might give up his purpose to his mother's pleadings if not to hers.   Friday, the widow paid her a visit.   After thanking Abby for certain gifts of preserves sent in during the week, she took out her handkerchief.

"You always have ben a good daughter to me, Abbylonia," she said; and the ready tears welled in her eyes.   "I cayn't say how I feel, I feel so for you in this hour of trial.   I 've made it a subjec' of prayer, and studied

and studied on it till my hand'cher wasn't
enough and I had to take my apron! And
this here is how I look at it. Abby, honey,
there ain't no good comes of fighting agin
the will of the Lord. I knew Eli hadn't no
call to be a minister. He knew it too, and
he tried to beg off; but I kept a-pecking at
him and a-worrying of him until he gave up,
wore out. And now looks like it is a judgment on me that he is going to quit in the
sight of men. I 've talked with him, and
he 's spoke his mind; and, Abby, I cayn't
oppose him, though it 'll mortify me so I
reckon I 'll be obliged to leave town."

Abby laid her sewing down. The widow
shielded herself behind her handkerchief
and sobbed. Had Abby scolded her, she
would have sobbed the louder. But Abby
answered, in a quiet, mild, voice: "I expect
you have aimed to do right, maw. I don't
want you to think I blamed you. It 's between Eli and me. Don't cry. Look at this
dress of Susy Nell's. Do you reckon she
will like it?"

The widow sniffed gratefully, and was
sure Susy Nell would like such a beautiful

frock.   She did not adventure any return to
the perilous theme, and soon fared forth,
equally bewildered and relieved.

Then Abby, in her neat street gown, her
smooth hair shining, and every pin on her
in place, walked down the broad, sunny village street, where bluets were sprinkling
the green sod on either side the wooden
walk, to Bud Slater's store, and bought a
box of rat poison, with a lying jest.   That
night, for the first time in a week, she slept
all night.   All day Saturday her manner
was exceedingly gentle.   Eli was moved by
her soft, unusual ways, but did not know
how to show his feeling, beyond constant
attention to the wood boxes and buying her
a copper wash boiler.   The strange diffi-
dence that often stands between those in
the closest relations, locked his tongue
while he longed to speak.   Abby no longer
cared to talk.   The desire for expression
was all burned out by the constant thought
of that one tremendous expression on which
she was resolved.

Sunday morning dawned bright and beautiful, as March mornings often dawn in Ar-

kansas.   Abby bathed and dressed herself with unusual care.   Then she made
Susy Nell ready for church.   She wondered at herself that she shouldn't feel more
— this last time she would ever dress the
child.   She kissed her, but there was neither
grief nor passion in the kiss.   That was because grief belonged to the left lobes of the
brain, and somehow it had become mis-
placed, and was on the right side; she
couldn't suffer on the right side.   " Or else
I'm a wicked woman who doesn't love her
children," thought Abby.   "I'll let her go
to Bessie Moon's for dinner.   Better for
her.   I'd like to see her once more, but it
doesn't matter about me; I'm a wicked woman.   The hill women used to love their
children best, better than their husbands,
but I always loved Eli best — better than
baby, even.   Baby, what are you crying
out in the barn for?   Oh, he bruised his
little pale cheek!   Oh, baby, baby! the
bruise was there in his coffin!   And Mrs.
Mitchell fetched all her flowers.   She came
over in that calico that was so short in
front — I wish I'd helped her cut that dress

instead of just lending her the pattern —
she came over in all the rain. I hated to
have it rain, and I cried that night to have
it raining on his little grave, and to have
him out in it all alone. I wish I could cry
now."

But she did not cry; after all, why should
she, when she would soon be out of all the
worry, and wouldn't need to feel her
thoughts beating through her brain?

It was a little difficult to remember about
the cooking; nevertheless, she did remember, and it was a better breakfast than common that she set before Eli. He ate very
little of it. She said to herself that a few
weeks ago she would have thought how
handsome and manly he looked in his new
black suit. Now she merely wondered
would he have it for his wedding suit when
he married again? Even that stab fluttered
her heart but a second; then she was back
working those weary thoughts through her
brain.

Eli started when she came into the room
ready for church. "It's awful kind of you,

Abby," he faltered, "but you don't need to go.   Maw is going to stay home."

"I rather go, Eli," said Abby, untenderly but gently.

They walked down the street together, little Susy Nell tripping ahead in the sunshine. The town was prosperous, and there were two or three new brick buildings with wooden trimmings smart with paint. Here and there over the plain a mansion rose a story or two above the pointed roofs; but for the most part the houses were modest southern cottages, not too finical about the back yards. The church bells were ringing, and the street was full of little groups of people wending their way churchward in sedate cheerfulness. The children's white frocks and a few lawn gowns lent a brightsome air to the simple toilettes.

Abby gazed quite carelessly about her. To-morrow—to-morrow—where would she be? She wondered why she did not suffer. "I'm going to die to-night, and I don't care," she said to herself, dully. "I reckon I'm past it." She didn't want to think, because it was such heavy work pushing the thoughts through the cells of her brain; and something seemed to be loose in the machinery within her head, and to be rattling about; but she kept remembering how after baby died Eli was in the same kind of daze. She, in her own passionate anguish, had called him stupid of heart. Perhaps she had misjudged him. It was then that the misunderstanding, the alienation, began between them. She had written a sermon about the death of children — a sermon that she seemed to write with the very blood of her heart — and Eli refused to preach it. He said: "I cayn't do it!" and when she pressed for a reason he answered, "I don't want to; it makes me feel too bad."

Her vanity was hurt. Without a word she wrote him another sermon, instead of the old one which he proposed to preach. She never mentioned the sermon afterward. Neither did he. Nor did she see it again; but she found some charred sheets of paper in the embers on the hearth next morning, and concluded (without examining) that Eli had burned the sermon overnight. And it hurt her.   But now that it was too late, now that everything was too late, she wondered whether she had not been rash and hard.   They were passing Colonel O'Neil's house, where the few Episcopalians of the village gathered Sundays to listen to the service read by one of their number.   The music of their hymn rose in an air plaintive and intense.   Passing the open window, Abby could hear every word:

> " In the hour of trial,
>   Jesus, plead for me!
>   Lest by base denial
>   I depart from Thee."

She stole a glance at Eli.   Was that the way *he* felt?   A new apprehension of his motives was struggling into her confused mind.   She drew a step nearer to him.   Eli turned his eyes on her.

" I expect the folks are anxious to see the new paint," said he.   " I spoke to Hobson and warned him, but he said he reckoned he knew his own business; and I 'm nigh certain he hasn't used hard finish.   Don't you sit down without feeling, Abby!"

Abby laughed a hard little laugh, and

said that she wouldn't. She did not speak again. She had wondered what was passing through his mind. Well, she knew now —in this supreme day of his life he was worrying about paint! No, she hadn't done him injustice.

Eli parted with her at the church door. "Abby," he began — "Abby" — and could get no further; but he put out his rough workingman's hand and touched her sleeve with a lingering fall. Then he smiled feebly, and ended, "Mind you look out for the paint."

She did not understand that he was yearning to express his own suffering and his sympathy for her, that he longed to touch her, as a child in pain longs to touch its mother. And she parted from him with a mortal ache in her heart. Yet his words followed her, trivial as they were, and automatically she obeyed them. She touched the seat of the pew, which, truly enough, was sticky; and before Susy Nell and she sat down, she covered back and seat with one of the Sunday school papers which were scattered among the pews. Then she seated herself, and sank into a dreary reverie, imageless and numb. When she glanced up the pews were full, and Sister Arnott, in all the pomp of her new gown, was stiffly inclining her shoulders as she sat down in the front pew. The indestructible respect of a woman for a pretty gown was stronger in Abby at that moment than her own misery, and far stronger than any ill will that she might bear to the wearer. Hastily she arrested the descent of those rustling sleeves. "Don't!" she whispered; "the varnish is all sticky; you 'll spoil your dress!" And she picked up a paper and spread it out herself. At the same moment she nodded a warning to three women who were entering the seat, behind. "Perhaps the other seats stick too," she said. But Sister Arnott, with dignity, replied that these seats were varnished last; the others would surely be dry. And Abby, caring little, sank back into her thoughts.

Eli was on his feet announcing the hymn. "We will sing the one hundred and fortieth hymn, on page twenty-five — No. 140, page

25. 'God moves in a mysterious way His wonders to perform.'" The words rolled back into the minister's throat. He could see the whole church. And decidedly it was a spectacle to be seen, for all over the church men and women were struggling to rise, and squirming helplessly, wrathfully, on their seats.

The climax came when a wailing childish voice pealed out: "Mamma! mamma! I' *stuck!*" Then the emotions that decorum had gagged burst forth. There was a rending sound, a buzz of voices. The children especially were in great power, little girls whimpering and little boys giggling, and Sister Wayling's baby bawling with fright. Men wrestled and women writhed, but the varnish held stanchly, and the scene became a wild one. Brother Arnott, who came a few minutes late, stood horror-stricken in the middle of the aisle. The minister hurried to the aid of his imprisoned flock. Sister Arnott, Abby, a few fortunate tardy sheep, the three women in the seat behind Abby, and perhaps half a dozen provident ones whose custom was to look before they sat as well as before they leaped, helped Brother Arnott and Eli to pull and twist and wrench the people free, although at a sad cost to their Sunday clothes. At last all except Sister Moon and Brother Tredith were rescued from the snare of the spoiler, and the congregation gathered about these captives. Sister Moon was a woman of weight in every sense, the richest personage in the town, with a rich vein of obstinacy running through a pious and kindly nature, who had long since ceased to tempt the scales. Brother Tredith was a man of substance and great stature, and (as he carefully explained) he had sat down "kinder sky west and crooked," hence there was the more of him to stick.

As for Sister Moon, she announced piteously to her audience: "It ain't that I'm so powerful heavy, but I always did set down hard! And, oh laws! this seat sticks like fly paper! I'll never have another sheet in my house, now I know how it feels! It's awful! Brother Eddings, nev' mind if you do tear my dress; I got plenty on underneath to be decent, and I never *was* proud!

Pull away! Bless you, Sister Eddings, I really felt it give a mite then. Cayn't some more ketch holt on me? Brother Eddings, it's all we-all's own fault, for you done told us, and told them to put on different varnish; I know if you'd 'a' painted this church we'd be standing free praising the Lord this minnit!"

And Brother Tredith's tolling base chimed in: "That's right! There ain't a better painter in Arkansas, whatever you call him for a preacher! Now most like we'll have to be soaked off with alcohol, and all Hobson's fool work!"

The tide thus started ran high against Hobson, at which no one could wonder who had what might be called an all-rouud view of the unfortunate congregation. By this time a charitable commercial traveler was trying the effect of whisky on varnish, under Brother Tredith's direction, and those around Sister Moon were weak with laughter. Eli himself gave the last pull which freed her, and was in time to peel off Brother Tredith's long legs. Then Abby reached him, and whispered him to dismiss the congregation, which he did in a single sentence, "I reckon we all better go home now."

Abby lingered a little time behind the others; she was detained by Sister Arnott. Sister Arnott had never liked Abby, but now she took her hand, saying, heartily, "Sister Eddings, I am ashamed I got this dress when I more than half suspected you wanted it; and I think you showed a right Christian spirit saving it for me; and if I can ever do anything for you, count on *me!*"

Abby smiled, and said something in reply, she hardly knew what. She had the sensation of a criminal who receives a reprieve on his journey to the gallows. Moreover, the whole drift of her mind was diverted violently by the farce of the paint. It seemed ridiculous to think of suicide when she was still laughing over the picture of Sister Moon! Almost unconsciously she found herself laughing at it with Eli. "I believe maw would have had to laugh too," she cried. "I wish she had been there."

"It was awful good of you to come this morning," said Eli, with a grateful look;

"and maw told me 'bout that dress, how you wanted it, and I sent to St. Louis for one for you. I think it was right sweet of you saving it for Sister Arnott that way."

"She looked so pretty in it, and it is such a nice dress —— "

Eli opened his mouth, gasping vainly; it seemed to him a very lame speech that he made, but perhaps it served his purpose with Abby quite as well as eloquence. He said: "You 're a heap prettier than her, Abby!"

Abby stood still in the road to look at him; but no suspicion could endure before his simple-hearted gaze. She reddened and smiled in spite of herself. "You haven't said that much to me, Eli, for—years!"

"But you knew I thought it!"

"No, I didn't. Susy Nell, run ahead; Bessie Moon's signaling to you over yonder! I reckon I am mean, Eli, but it 's mighty hard to have your husband think so —— "

"I never did think so, as God hears me, honey. But you were so much smarter 'n me, and wrote such beautiful sermons, I 'lowed you looked down on a uneducated man like me —— "

"Eli" — his wife interrupted him in strong agitation — "Eli, I believed you despised *me* because — because I wrote the sermons for you!"

He was in front of the puddle which had disturbed the widow; in his excitement he splashed into the worst of it. "I ain't such a pusillanimous, ornery, trifling tyke as that," he cried. "Abby, forgive me; I am pulling you into the mud!"

"You can pull me through all the mud in Hickory Ridge, Eli Eddings, and I won't say one word!"

He swung around. His eyes kindled. He caught the little figure up in his arms and carried her across the puddle to the firm ground. As he put her down he made a shamefaced apology: "Abby, I was just naturally *obliged* to get hold of you and hug you, and I didn't see no other way, out in the street as we are!"

Abby only made a kind of gurgle in her throat, and ran swiftly through their gate down the walk to the house. But when he overtook her, in their little parlor, simple as he was in woman's moods, he understood that his wife was not angry with him.

He sat down, he drew his wife on his knee in the fashion of his early married life, and kissed her. "Abby," said he, "I feel now like I could tell you all about it. You know how come I went into the ministry. I hadn't no more call to it than our caff! I went to please maw and you. And I staid because *you* wanted me! Oh, Abby" — his voice melted, and she hid her face — "*you* know what I felt about you! Why, your very clothes were so much nicer than the other girls', and the way you wore your hair, and it 's white on your neck where the hair grows, and when I was near you I felt like I was walking in the woods with the wild honeyseckles! Abby! Abby! you little thing that I could crush, you 're just like a flower yourself, honey, dearie. Don't cry, honey; I cayn't go on and do what I had ought to do if you cry; I 'll *have* to give in to you, I love you so!"

And Abby? She forgot the nightmare of the last week, she forgot how she hated to

live in the country, she forgot everything
except that her husband loved her, and she
sobbed, "Oh, Eli, I 'll go anywhere and I 'll
live anyhow if you only will love me like
that!"

"I love you a hundred thousand times
better than you know, Abby," he cried.
"Why, dearie, it was you converted me and
made me give up preaching. What you
trembling so for, lambie? Listen; it was
this way: I read your sermons, and they
worked on me. It was slow, for I 'm slow.
I don't know how to talk out things even to
myself, and that makes me slow. But they
worked on me. Abby, there was one sermon—you wrote it ayfter little Eli died——"

"Yes," said Abby, in a tense voice.

"I didn't seem to know where I was or
what I was doing those days. I — I felt very
bad, Abby."

Abby's hand stroked his brown curls,
trembling; she could not speak.

"When I read that sermon, for the first
time I could cry. And I was out in the
willows by the river, and I kneeled right
down and prayed to the Lord to have mercy

and show me the way out and comfort us both! Abby, He will. But I couldn't preach that sermon."

"What did you do with it, Eli?"

"Wait a minute," said he. He put her out of his arms very tenderly, and went out of the room, while she waited for him, trembling.

She heard his footsteps moving about their chamber; they came back again. He was standing before her with the neat square sheets that she knew in his hands. And she read on the outside, in Eli's cramped hand, "*This sermon, which I thank God for, was written by my dear wife after the death of our dear son Eli.*" There followed the date.

"Now you know," said Eli, "how you converted me. Ayfter that I felt I couldn't live a lie before you. But I wasn't strong enough, knowing the anxious notion you had of me being a minister, to stop right away, and I waited till I got things fixed so I can get a shop in this town; and you shall have the same money you had for the preaching, and more if you will take it, and we 'll get a hired girl, so you 'll have time to read your books; and, Abby, when it fell out this way this morning, I said to myself, 'Maybe the Lord ain't requiring a public confession of you, and maybe I could just say I didn't feel myself fitted, and quit.' What do you think, Abby?"

"I think," said Abby, "I 'd go over to Brother Arnott and tell *him* all, and abide by his decision."

"I will," cried Eli, with a deep intake of breath. "I 'll go now while you 're getting dinner. Say, Abby, in your drawer on your bureau was standing this that you got for the rats; don't you think it 's kinder dangerous having it there? Susy Nell —— "

Abby caught it out of his hand and hurled the box into the open fire. "Yes, yes," said she; "it 's a wicked thing. You go, Eli. And, Eli, you go tell your mother before you come home!" Then, as his footsteps echoed on the wooden walk, she sank lower and lower, and kneeled before the chair where he had sat.

The Ladder of Grief

The Ladder of Grief.

❧

Through love to light! Oh, wonderful the way
That leads from darkness to the perfect day!
—*Richard Watson Gilder.*

THERE was a great deal of sympathy in Fairport for Mr. Markham when his wife died. Silas Markham was the president of the principal bank, a man respected by every one, although he had no intimate friends. He was a just man; in many ways he was merciful, and he would keep his word to his hurt; but there was about him always a reserve, a species of coldness, building a barrier beyond which, to the knowledge of Fairport, only one human being had ever passed. This one person was his wife. His love for her the very servants in the house knew; and they served him the better for it, because they all loved her.

Now that, after a few hours' illness, and a
swift unconsciousness that never lifted, the
wife had slipped out of the world with no
last words, she who would not have dismissed a beggar ungently, and he was left
alone in his desolate house, unconsoled by
so much as the memory of a last embrace,
his sorrow was of a kind that any one could
pity. Yet, really, no one knew its compass.
During those first stunned weeks he hardly
realized it himself; but now it was coming
to him with every day, with every horrible
night. Markham was a man of will. He
had no more mind to be crazy than he had
to seek an ignoble and brutal forgetfulness
of his torment in drink or opium. Yet
night after night he slept only to dream one
hideous dream. He was always seeking
Agnes. The night damp would be in his
hair, and the dream chill in his heart, as
he would wander over a vast and treeless
prairie trying to find. his wife, while the
faint light on the edge of the horizon faded.
He never found her. Always he woke up
in a dreadful fright at the darkness and
something horrible which was about to

happen. And awake, he would put out his hand and remember, but have no tears to relieve his scorched heart. One day he said to himself, "I *must* get nearer to her, somehow, or I shall go mad!" He was sitting, as he used to sit of an evening, in his library, the neglected newspapers littering the desk, his head sunk on his breast, thinking. Rather, one should say, dreaming, since thought is too orderly a word for that dreary and aimless drift of past scenes. At intervals his numbed will would struggle to tear him away from the wretched panorama, but it was not strong enough to hold him; he always harked back to it, and was living over again moments bitter or sweet.

The library was a beautiful room. It was she that chose all the books; she that planned the great mullioned window and the fireplace, and the somber richness of furniture. "This is to be *your* room, Si," she had said. "I'm going to make it to represent you; it is to be characteristic."

"But why not represent you, too?" said he.

"The whole house represents me," she smiled back, "you are so indulgent!"

"Am I?" he asked lightly. She flushed; her eyelids fell.

"I never asked for but one thing you didn't grant me," said she; and her eyes for one troubled instant questioned his. But he made no answer. He knew what she meant, but felt no desire to discuss this one point of variance; and perhaps her courage was exhausted when she mentioned it. Aggie was not a daring woman. How the color would dapple her cheek, her pretty oval cheek, when she tried to say something; and she never could hold her sweet voice even. But how brave she was, too! When the children were born, the poor little babies that died, it was *he* was the coward; she —— He broke down, remembering. It was well; it was good for him to cry. Then he looked at her picture above the desk. A great artist had painted it. Why had the fellow made her look so sad? The babies' deaths were hard to bear; but it was five years since little Silas died, and *he* was still with her, and she loved him —

surely she loved him; surely he made her
happy. Yet that crank had made her
lovely dark eyes so wistful, and her smile
was sadder than tears. It was ridiculous
to imagine that the one thing about which
they differed, which neither of them, by
tacit consent, ever mentioned, could have
been a shadow on her life. He turned rest-
lessly away from the canvas, and tried to
fix his attention on the plans for the children's hospital which he was building as a
memorial of his wife. But almost immediately he pushed the neat parchment rolls
away, and his head sank on his hands.

"If I could only dream of her," groaned
the lonely man; "she said she would come
to my dreams."

As married lovers will, they had talked
of the dread possibility of loneliness. She
had introduced the subject, and he had
checked her, clasping her almost roughly
to his heart, crying, "I couldn't *live* without you!" But smiling with a thrill, over
his violence, she had continued, "Si, I
would come back to you; we should be so

near. I could get back to your dreams, I know."

"Near?" he murmured.

"I believe"—and now she was pressing her face close to his heart, and he could not see it—"I believe I could come. You know what the theosophists think, and don't you remember that lovely book of Du Maurier's and those two lovers who could 'dream true'? It was because their souls were so near—like ours."

The remembrance of that promise came to him as he knelt by a still form and talked, half-crazed, to his dead wife the whole night through. "I'll get near enough, Aggie; you'll see, you'll see!" he had whispered, stroking her hair with his gentlest touch. To-night his lip curled and his heart was ice as he retraced his efforts to get nearer to Aggie. Once he had gone to a limp, scared little spiritual medium whose husband rented rooms in one of his buildings, and he had sat on a dingy plush sofa, and watched the sunbeams gild the dust on a rickety table and a strange woman behind the table "acting

Aggie," until he sickened of the profanity. At the end of the second "trance" he rose and handed the medium a bank note, the figure on which sent the blood into her sallow cheeks.

"I think this will pay you for your trouble, madam," he said; "I shall not come any more." The medium hoped that the communications had given him comfort, and was sorely puzzled by his reply: "No, ma'am. But I think I understand." With which, and a solemn bow, he fared forth from her presence, and the red plush sofa and the dusty table knew him no more.

"It wasn't Aggie" — so he summed up his experience — "though she told things only Aggie and I knew; but she didn't tell anything outside my thoughts; and I had no business, I nor any other decent man, to go where my thoughts of my wife could be pulled out of me."

The same harassing longing for a spiritual sense of his wife's presence sent him to her church, although he did not like either the church or the rector. The church was "high"; and to Markham, the pagan son of

Puritan parents, the ritual of the church was merely a spectacle, tawdry or tedious, according to the pomp with which it was presented. The rector was a young man whose earnest soul would have moved his western auditors more had it not been expressed with an English accent. Markham put no objections in his wife's path, but he stayed home and read the papers. When Mrs. Markham died, the parish sorely missed her open hand. Therefore, when, one Sunday, a tall, erect, thin man, with a beautiful gray head and a profile fine and stern enough for a Roman coin, walked composedly down the aisle after the flock of crumpled cottas, the rector's pulses bounded. Markham was so rich, and, were he so minded, he could be so generous; and they were so poor!

The rector kept his hopes under cover, but the senior warden said frankly: "I do hope you can hold him; there's no telling what he'll do if we can get him interested."

Six Sundays the rector held him, during which time gradually the listener came to exert a singular and sinister influence over the preacher.   He felt himself dogged from the versicles to the benediction by a baffling sense of failure.   He unfolded the beauties of the higher life and the mystic helpfulness of the church services with all the ardor of young zeal; and the rigid shape in the Markham pew, which neither rose nor knelt, the immovable, attentive, unresponsive countenance bent on him, while the man sat with his wife's hymnal unopened in his hand, turned into a kind of a specter of the skepticism of the whole world.   The preacher's studied arguments and his eager, boyish appeals beat against the man of the world's indifference as helplessly as a child's fists beat against a locked door.   It bewildered, then it disconcerted him; in the end, it nearly palsied his tongue.   The Sunday that saw the Markham pew empty, saw the rector, amid his humiliation and dismay at the vision of the senior warden's reproaches, drawing a guilty sigh of relief. After all, there was no fear of the senior warden; he was in high feather over Markham's farewell check; he congratulated the rector heartily.

"He came to see what he thought of us; and it is plain he thought that we deserved his wife's interest," declared the senior warden. "I guess he sees now there is something in the High Church besides candles and a boy choir. And that reminds me, don't you think we could afford to have the boys' cottas done up twice a month now? They do look pretty mussy by the fourth Sunday."

And Markham was sitting at his library desk gazing wearily at the plans for the hospital. "Everything fails," he said; "this will fail, too, I suppose. Why doesn't Wheatly come?"

Like an answer the heavy door opened, and Milly, the waitress, glided into the room with the lugubrious mien that was her own tribute of sympathy, and in a hushed voice announced: "Mr. Wheatly, sir. Shall I fetch him in here?"

Wheatly had been Markham's lawyer for years; he might almost be called an intimate friend. "Markham's got a heart somewhere," he often assured his wife, "and any day I'm liable to find it." He was a tall man, of a dignified portliness, with a noble bald head and shrewd blue eye. He joyed in battle, and bullied jury and judge alike, and, one may say, won his cases with a sledge hammer; but nobody charged smaller fees to poor clients, or could be gentler to the friendless and undefended.

He greeted Markham, and plunged at once into the business of their meeting. They settled the details of the deeds in entire harmony; but, the business concluded, Wheatly fidgeted in his chair, puffing hard on his Henry Clay, and twice opening his lips and shutting them again, in the manner of the man who oscillates between speech as good and silence as better. Suddenly he said brusquely, "Markham, my wife says I ought to tell you something."

"Mrs. Wheatly is always right," said Markham, with his dry politeness.

"You see, Markham, we have known Mrs. Markham ever since she was a little girl—why, I taught her to ride her first pony, in the old major's time——"

"And do you think I shall ever forget how kind you were when the major died and they were left without anything?"

"That was nothing. What I meant to say was that Agnes naturally felt to us almost as if she had been a niece or such a relation, and — and she used to talk to us about her friends the Haskills. I fancy," said the lawyer, carefully watching the glowing ash of his cigar, "that we were the only people to whom she did say anything about them. She was rather anxious about Mrs. Haskill's health. She hasn't been well. The fact is, that woman works too hard. She makes light of it, but she has worked her strength all out. Agnes was deeply attached to Mrs. Haskill, you know. And one day she asked me to draw up her will. It was the day before she was taken ill, and perhaps she didn't have time to tell you about it."

Markham bent to pick up a paper weight which clattered to the oaken floor. He wore his face of wood. "She did not tell me," said he.

"Well," — the lawyer found it easier not

to look at his friend as he spun off the items of the will — "she left a list of friends to whom she wished you to give keepsakes out of her jewels. I think you have anticipated her wishes there; I know you have with us."

"If you will give me the list, I will attend to it," said Markham in an emotionless tone.

"She left some money to each of the servants."

"I have given each of them a hundred dollars. I thought of that myself," said Markham.

"She left a thousand dollars to the church, St. Anne's, and five hundred to the rector."

"I sent five thousand to the church; I'll attend to the rector," said Markham.

"She left five hundred to the hospital, for a children's ward."

Markham silently laid his finger tips on the heap of architect linen, with its neat drawings in colored inks.

"All the residue of her estate she left to Emma Haskill."

Did he expect any sign of feeling from

his client? Markham gave none whatever. For a second there was silence; Wheatly puffed on his cigar and looked at the portrait. The wistful eyes met his. He strangled a sigh.

"She didn't sign the will?" said Markham.

"No; I simply took her instructions for it, and she was to come in another time. It's so much waste paper—legally." Markham lighted a fresh cigar; but Wheatly noticed that a good half of a cigar was charring on the table beside the paper weight.

"I'm afraid Haskill is in pretty bad shape," said he. "He was on Keene's bond, and the runaway has done him up; he will lose his house and every dollar he has in the world. It's too bad. Ralph's an honest man, though he belongs to the class that always bet on the losing horse. As for Emma Haskill"—Wheatly looked at this instant just as he looked when he dominated the court room, and gave the judge to understand both law and justice were on his side, wherever His Honor might be found—"I don't know a better woman."

"Wheatly," said Markham," she is the only woman in the world whom I dislike."

"I was afraid of that," said Wheatly.

"My wife and I never had but one difference. That was about her. She was a school girl friend of Aggie's. She had great influence over her. I never liked her, but I was civil. We held different opinions on every subject, and she didn't in the least conceal what she thought; she is one of those loud-voiced, shrieking women who like to argue. I didn't care to argue with her, so avoided meeting her. I told Agnes frankly that I didn't like being schooled by her friend; the house was as much hers as mine, but I should be obliged if she would choose those hours to invite Mrs. Haskill when I could be absent. Unluckily, Mrs. Haskill overheard me, and she chose, later, to make a scene with Aggie, and refused to enter the house again. Agnes cried herself sick over the episode, and that didn't make me feel any more kindly toward the woman. Aggie used to go there, and she was always doing things for them; but I saw nothing of them. Once — after

—after our little boy died, she asked me could she have that oldest girl of the Haskills', the one they named after her, up to the house for a two weeks' visit. I said she could. But I went away that night and stayed for two weeks. I made a pretense of sudden business. She never asked for the child again. But she was always going to see them and giving them things." He set his teeth on the next sentence and stopped. Milly softly opened the door, she softly stole into the room, and, nodding her head gloomily, announced in the lowest of voices that use the vocal chords, "Mr. Haskill begs you'll see him a moment as a great favor, sir."

"Very well; I'll see him — here," said Markham.

Wheatly rose; he had no choice but to make his farewell. Nevertheless, as he told his wife, he felt that that well meaning idiot would kick over the whole bucket of fish.

For a few minutes Markham was left alone. He was facing a grotesque and horrible dilemma, for he was angry with his dead wife. To be angry and rage futilely is an ugly pain; but to be angry with the dead that we love, to know that they can never hear our reproaches or justify themselves and put us in the wrong — this wrings the soul! For, however angry we may be with them while alive, we have always, under our anger, the hope that they have not wronged our love, and that it is we, not they, who will need to be forgiven. But Agnes could never explain. There was left him — yes, there was one thing left him; and his mind darted to a purpose bearing little good for the man in the hall.

"Good evening, Mr. Markham," said a deprecating voice. Markham did not take the pains to smile. He was on his feet already, therefore he did not rise. Haskill extended a hand that fell instantly, Markham busying himself in pushing a chair at his visitor.

"What can I do for you this evening Mr. Haskill?" said he. Haskill sat down on the edge of the chair, a great leathern armchair that looked ready to engulf him entirely. He was a small man, prematurely bald, wrinkled under the eyelids. His skin was fair, flushing readily, and (in Markham's opinion) he was prone to equally irrational fever fits of fear and hope. In his early manhood he had inherited a small fortune, promptly lost in headlong ventures. Since then he had been a clerk in a dry goods shop, advancing no farther than the silk counter, although every one liked to trade with Ralph Haskill. He had made a careful toilet, the sight of which had given him a flicker of confidence as he stood before the mirror at home; but now, while Markham's cold eye traveled from the shiny seam of the left elbow to the neatest of patches in the hem of his right trouser leg (why must he have tried to learn to ride a wheel when he had on his good clothes?), he felt suddenly poor and shabby — the man who had failed begging of the man who had succeeded. His tongue grew too large for his dry throat. "I have come to — to ask a favor of you, Mr. Markham," he said.

"So I presumed," said Markham. It was not an encouraging beginning of the interview.

"I shouldn't want you to call it exactly a favor, either," said Haskill, struggling not to seem so dejected as he was. "I am sure, Mr. Markham, little as you may like me, you are a just man."

"I don't see what my liking or disliking you has to do with that," said Markham, cruelly at his ease.

Haskill forced the quivering muscles of his mouth into a smile. "Of course, it hasn't; but I mean I think you wouldn't let any prepossession against me make—make you decide unjustly."

"No?" said Markham.

"This is the case with me," said Haskill, gulping down something in his throat: "my wife is sick. She's worked like a dog for me and the children. God knows I've tried to make money, but either I'm too honest or I'm too stupid or I get to believing in the wrong things. Whatever's the reason, we haven't got on; and my wife's done everything, Mr. Markham. She's scrubbed the floors, she's worked in the garden, she's made the children's clothes, she's gone without a girl when there were two babies.

together, and —always so cheerfully —— "
He choked, and his eyes filled, but he
straightened the quiver in his voice, going
on quickly: "The doctor says she must go
to Colorado. It isn't — there's no hemor-
rhage; and, besides, they cure consumption
nowadays. He told me he'd engage she
would be well to go this winter and rest. If
Aggie—if my oldest girl could go with her,
and they needn't travel poor, but have a
section in a sleeper and board in a comfortable place — I know she'd get well. I
haven't anything to raise money on or I
wouldn't come to you, Mr. Markham; but
you know about Keene. My house and the
few hundreds we had saved — they're all
gone. It's my wife's life at stake, Mr.
Markham——" For the first time his haggard eyes interrogated Markham's, and the
anguish in him overflowed. "Mr. Markham, you've lost your wife; you know what
it is. I can't sleep nights, I'm so worried.
And the doctor's sure she'll get well if she
can go." Markham's brow wrinkled, which
meant that he was moved; he couldn't tell,
himself, whether it was irritation or a faint

rousing of pity. But his mind was so filled with its tumult of anger and suspicion that the other feeling could not edge into the crowd. Yet it did stand outside; he did perceive its presence. Poor Haskill desperately blundered on: "I wouldn't have ventured to ask such a favor, but it isn't as a favor. Emma says we've the right to tell you the truth. It's this way, Mr. Markham. Aggie" (Markham shut his teeth at the familiar diminutive of his wife's name), "Aggie came to our house the very week before she died, and she was talking with Emma, and she told Emma she ought to go south this winter, and she said, 'I'll see you go, Emma,' says she, 'and if anything happens to me, you'll find I haven't forgotten you and little Aggie.' Those were her very words."

"What you mean is that my wife meant to leave you money in her will?" said Markham.

"Yes, sir," said Haskill; and he gripped the arms of his chair with both hands.

"I suppose you know every cent she had I gave her. She died without making a will.

The money coming back thus to my hands by law, do you think I am bound to pay it out?"

"Didn't you give it to her?" said Haskill. The sweat beaded his pale face; his eyes were wild.

"He is suffering," Markham thought; but the thought, like his transient pity, was outside a fixed intention which seemed to possess him.

"Didn't you give it to her for her own — not to take back?" cried Haskill.

"Yes, I gave it to her for her own," said Markham.

"And wouldn't you think that what she wanted, you ought to do, even — even if she was dead?"

"Yes," said Markham, "I would. Let me ask you a question. Would you think my obligation ended there?"

"I don't understand you, sir; maybe I'm stupid — or it's being so — so anxious."

Markham frowned again. "I mean, do you think I am bound to do any more than divide what property my wife left according to her wishes, so far as I know them?"

"No, sir. If you divide Aggie's money as she wished, what more could we ask?"

"Well, you might ask that *I*, out of my own money, should give what she wanted given."

"Certainly not, sir. It is only what she left —— "

"I don't intend to take one cent of any money left by Mrs. Markham," said Markham, looking full at Haskill; and, somehow, in spite of the reassuring words, the man felt his heart curdle within him. "But, Mr. Haskill, do you know how Mrs. Markham invested that money? *You* had faith in Keene; he gave you a commission. You wanted her to invest —— "

"She put that money with Keene?" Haskill's voice was not more than a whisper. "You — you let her?"

"As you have said, Mr. Haskill, it was her money; I let her."

Haskill shrank back in his chair. "Is it all gone?" said he.

"All, I think."

An instinct that he did not recognize averted his eyes from the crushed creature

in the chair.   He half wished — but Haskill
was on his feet; he was speaking; and it
was queer that his voice should be firmer
than it had been yet.   "I 'll not trouble
you longer, Mr. Markham.   I hope — I hope
Aggie did not know."

"No, she didn't know."

Haskill said, "I 'm glad for that," and
would have walked out of the room; at the
door he tottered.

"You 're not well!" said Markham, touching the decanter on the desk.   "A glass of
wine?"

But Haskill, with almost a glance of
horror, waved him aside.   Then, the swing
of the door in his ears, Markham remembered some stories of Haskill's youth, before he married.   "He might find that beastly sort of oblivion more tempting than I,"
he thought.   He turned away.   He looked
at the picture.   His heart was numb.   "O
Aggie, come back, come back and tell me
why you did it!" he cried, stretching out
his hands.   And even as he spoke, his wrath
was cut off like the foam upon the water.
He had driven straight toward his fero-

cious purpose, under the first sting of his knowledge; but now that he had transferred his torture to another soul he was seized with a sick disgust of his own cruelty. It was base in him to stand by in his perverse pride and let Aggie fling her little fortune away. "When I hoped she would lose it and find out what a crazy loon he was, and it would make a coolness between them!" he cried. He had prided himself coldly that he was a just man. Was it just to punish his wife through these humble people that she loved? "I suppose," he said aloud — he was getting into a silly habit of talking to himself; it was part of his distempered state now that he had lost his only confidant — "I suppose I was jealous. I wasn't afraid that she loved Emma Haskill as she loved me; I knew better. Aggie, I knew, I knew how you loved me; but I was jealous because you didn't love me so absorbingly that you would give up anything that I asked you to, just because I asked you. If you had been willing, I would not have demanded it." Then he returned to every inflection of Haskill's voice and every motion and change of expression in his pitiful face. "The man," he muttered, "is suffering like me! He loves his wife, too!" He did not despise Haskill the less, but he began to pity a pain that was in the similitude of his own. Markham was a man of narrow imagination, and therefore he was an untender man in general; but here he could picture with a frightful vividness exactly the frame of mind of this other husband to whom he had just denied his wife's life. "Confound her! He shall have her if he wants her so infernally bad," he burst out at last, "if my money can give her to him."

All night he tore his soul with new doubts and fears. The light was stealing into the luxurious room before he threw himself on the lounge and sank into a dead and dreamless sleep. "I wish I could get that poor devil word he doesn't need to worry," was his last conscious thought. His first in the morning was a relief that the night had gone and he had not dreamed his nightmare dream. His next, that he would not prolong Haskill's suspense. Not waiting for

his breakfast, to the inexpressible conster-
nation of the servants, he was seen walking swiftly down the street before eight
o'clock — not twenty minutes after he was
awake.

The Haskill house was in the upper part
of the town, where land was cheaper.   The
house was of a familiar type — where the
ambitious architect strives for a large Colo-
nial effect with a dwelling of eight rooms,
mostly hall and piazza, but picturesque.
There was a tiny yard.   Even in early No-
vember the lawn was like green velvet.

A girl of ten was sweeping the porch.
Her motions had the deftness of long practice.   On the porch railing was perched a
very shabby canton flannel elephant.   Having swept the walk to the gate, the little
girl lifted the elephant and kissed it.   " You
've been real good," said she; "now we 'll
go in, and you can watch me make a sponge
cake all myself."   At this point Markham
opened the gate.

"Is this Mr. Haskill's?" he said, lifting
his hat with the ceremonious courtesy that
was easier to him than another man 's un-

dress manners, "and are you Mr. Haskill's little girl?"

"Yes, sir, I am Aggie Haskill," answered the girl.   She was a pretty little girl, Markham thought; her blue eyes and long lashes, and her fair, freckled face were like her father's.

"Is your mother in, Miss Aggie?"

"No, sir; she's gone to the grocery to get some eggs.   She told me to ask any one that I didn't know to sit down on the porch. Will you sit down, sir?   Papa's gone down town."

Evidently she did not know him.   It occurred to him that it was not quite the usual thing that the children of a woman's dearest friend, living in the same town, should not know her husband by sight. The Haskills had not forced themselves on his presence.   That, at least, might be said of Emma Haskill.   They had kept to their own side of the fence.   He came up to the piazza, and addressed himself to the child.

"What is your doll's name, little girl?" said he.

She drew out the elephant proudly.   "It

is not a doll, it's an elephant, and its name is Silas."

Markham experienced a queer surprise. "How's that? That's my name too."

The little girl smiled. "It's named after you, then, too. My Aunt Aggie made it. She made it for Johnny. That's my little brother. He's in heaven now. It had a red blanket, and a little basket all full of money; and Johnny wanted to call it after Aunt Aggie, only he couldn't, because it was a boy elephant, you know; so Aunt Aggie said why not call it after the one she loved best? and his name was Silas. So we called it Silas Markham, to be after her, too, you know."

"It's a very nice elephant. May I hold it?" said Markham. He held it carefully, stroking the flannel. His hand trembled a little.

"Silas was in a fire once," the little girl prattled away. She quite enjoyed being treated like a grown-up person by this polite gentleman.

"Indeed, how was that?" said Markham.

"It was this way: The house took fire.

It was at night, too, and we all had to run out; and when we were all out, Mamie began to cry because she had left Silas. He was sleeping with her that night, and she said, 'Oh, Si will burn! Si 's in there!' and so papa ran back, and a fireman ran with him. He was mad when he found it was only an elephant, but papa told him how it used to belong to his little boy that was dead, and then he said, 'Oh, that!' and was real kind. Si wasn't hurt a bit. We used to pretend to make him tell us how he felt when he was in the fire. It 's only pretend, of course."

Markham nodded. He was looking through the door into the little parlor. It almost seemed to him that he could detect his wife's gifts scattered among the plain furnishings.

"Did you know my Aunt Aggie?" asked the little girl.

"Yes," said Markham.

"She is in heaven," said the little girl, reverently. "I 'm named after her, and mamma says I must be a very good little girl like her. She was so good, and she looked so sweet. Sometimes I used to go riding with her in her carriage."

"Yes," said Markham.

"She was the best friend mamma had. When she died papa cried too. He got some flowers at the greenhouse. He didn't send them to the house, though, but mamma and he went up to the cemetery and put them on the grave. Oh, they were just beautiful flowers!"

Markham knew. He had seen the flowers laid on the mound. He wished that he had sent for Mrs. Haskill on the day of Aggie's death. When she came Aggie was dead; he had gone out of the chamber, leaving her there; he remembered how he had resented the sound of her sobs. "She had a right to grieve, too," he perceived for the first time. "I wish——"

"There's mamma," exclaimed the child, running out to joyously fall upon a tall woman with a basket on her arm.

Years and struggle and sorrow had tamed the exuberant young creature that Markham used to dislike. Her red cheeks were gone, and her bounding step dragged; but there was left her ready smile, which faded instantly as she perceived her caller. She greeted him courteously. He made no prelude to his errand.

"Haskill was to see me last night," said he; "after he left I considered the matter. Whatever Agnes wished to have done with her property I feel myself bound to do. The property is gone."

"Yes, I know," said Mrs. Haskill. She had not a loud voice to-day, and all her embarrassing vivacity was gone.

"I feel the obligation just the same," said Markham. "I shall send you a check for the sum at once."

Emma Haskill gasped. She was quite pale. "You are a very just man, Silas Markham," faltered she.

"Not always," said Markham; "but I want to do what she wished."

"You made her very happy." She was amazed at the wistful look in his eyes, and at his "Thank you" and his proffered hand.

Something prompted her, an impulsive woman, to say, "Won't you come again, some time, Mr. Markham?" Yet she was surprised to hear, instead of the expected formal thanks, "I will come. I want to take this little girl out to drive — with the elephant."

But she was not more surprised than he that he should be saying such words. And a stranger surprise still it was, that the first sentence uttered by any one that seemed even for the least space to lift the load on his heart should have come from Emma Haskill. Nor, later in the day, did he find any fault with Ralph Haskill, although he hated a display of emotion, and Haskill was crying like a baby.

"I felt like killing myself last night," Haskill sobbed. "I did think of it, but I couldn't leave her while she needed me; and this morning Mr. Wheatly offered to lend me the money —— "

"You won't need to borrow," said Markham; "the extra check, besides the legacy, is for the journey. Mrs. — my wife would have wanted Mrs. Haskill to have every comfort. You would better go with her this winter, all of you. I have seen about that. You can have a vacation. Don't be worried. Mrs. Haskill will come back all right."

Haskill wrung his hand. He had not a word.

With Markham, perhaps, it was as well. The latter halted at the door and said, without looking at Haskill, "I should like — I should feel obliged if — occasionally — you would let your little girl come to see me."

Then he went home. He opened the library door with the familiar sinking of his heart. But he did not, at once, look at his wife's picture, as was his custom. He sat down by his desk. He took out a list from his pocket, and noted something opposite each name.

"Whether it hurts me or not," he muttered, "no matter."

Next, he wrote a letter, a stiff business letter, inclosing a check. It was addressed to the rector of St. Anne's.

"Aggie, I 've done everything now," said he. As he spoke, he was fumbling among the stationery in the drawer for an envelope; hence it happened that his fingers

fell on his wife's portfolio. He had not
suspected that it was in the drawer. It
was the same dainty little affair of Russia
leather and silver that he had often seen in
his wife's lap; and he remembered how he
used to make small jokes about her un-
workmanlike manner of writing. He laid
the portfolio open on the table. A letter
was lying before him. " My dear, dear
husband" — the room reeled a little, but he
was reading quite calmly, only the back of
his head seemed to throb, and it was hard
for him to breathe.

My Dear, Dear Husband: I did something
to-day, and I want to tell you about it, but I haven't
the courage to talk to you. I went to Mr. Wheatly
to have him draw up my will. I didn't sign it,
dear; I wouldn't do such a thing without consult-
ing you. But he has it all drawn up, so that if I
were to be very ill I could sign it at a moment's
notice. Dear Silas, there has never been but one
thing to come between us. You did not like Emma
Haskill. To every other friend of mine you were
kind and good, but you were hardly civil to her;
and you know that she overheard what you said.
She never has been in the house since then. How
could she come? It hurts me—Oh, Si, it hurts me
so, that you two, who are the best and noblest per-

sons in the world, should have misunderstood each other so, and it seems as if it must be somehow my fault. Emma has been having such a hard time. I have tried to help her. But life is so uncertain, and I thought that I ought to make my will. But I know that you will value more the expression of my wishes than any legal document. And I felt I was treating you unkindly and undutifully, acting this way with the money which you have given me. So, instead, darling, will you pardon me for doing this without telling you? And I will go to Mr. Wheatly, and ask him to draw up a memorandum which I will enclose in this. We have been so happy, Silas, although we have had such sorrows; but there never has been but this one cloud on our love. I haven't been the wife I ought to have been to you; I am so silly and cowardly — not what your wife should be; but, oh, I *have* loved you! I am going to put this with my treasures. You will find it with every line that you ever wrote me, from that first note, asking if you might take mamma and me to the theater (how good, good, *good*, you were to mamma, and how often I have been grateful to you!) to your last dear letter. I do not know when you will find it; I hope you won't *need* to find it, because I mean to snuggle up to you, some evening, out on the porch, when it is dark, and whisper it all to you, and beg you to be kind and forgive. But, since I don't know what may happen, I will write this — perhaps we shall read it together. In the little time that may ——

Here the letter ended. Something had interrupted the writer, and she had pushed the sheet aside, never to finish it nor to have that one hour of confidence which should sweep every doubt away. Markham's tears were dropping fast, not for himself, but for her who had loved him, and yet had been lonely, struggling to be loyal to her old ties. Oh! if she had been lonely then, was he not lonely now? Yet, in that moment of repentance and grief, there came to him a strange foreshadowing of comfort. Out of the grave she had explained and put him in the wrong. He went up to the picture so close that he could touch the painted cheek with his hand. The eyes looked at him, and he found in them more love than sorrow. "Dearest," he whispered, "I'll try to be good to *all* your friends. I'll try to do what you would have done."

That night he dreamed of his wife.

The Captured Dream

The Captured Dream

Too late I have found thee, O beauty most ancient, O beauty most new!—*S. Augustine.*

SOMERS rode slowly over the low Iowa hills, fitting an air in his mind to Andrew Lang's dainty verses. Presently, being quite alone on the country road, he began to sing:

"Who wins his love shall lose her;
Who loses her shall gain;
For still the spirit wooes her,
A soul without a stain;
And mem'ry still pursues her,
With longings not in vain.

"He loses her who gains her,
Who watches day by day
The dust of time that stains her,
The griefs that leave her gray,
The flesh that yet enchains her,
Whose grace hath passed away.

" Oh, happier he who gains not
    The love some seem to gain;
The joy that custom stains not
    Shall still with him remain,
The loveliness that wanes not,
    The love that ne'er can wane.

" In dreams she grows not older,
    The land of dreams among,
Though all the world wax colder,
    Though all the songs be sung;
In dreams doth he behold her,
    Still fair and kind and young."

The gentle strain of melancholy and
baffled desire faded into silence, but the
young man's thoughts pursued it. A memory of his own that sometimes stung him,
sometimes plaintively caressed him, stirred
in his heart, "I am afraid you hit it, Andy,"
he muttered, "and I should have found it
only a dream had I won."

At thirty Somers fancied himself mighty
cynical. He consorted with daring critics,
and believed the worst both of art and of
letters. He was making campaign cartoons
for a daily journal instead of painting the
picture of the future; the panic of '93 had
stripped him of his little fortune, and his

sweetheart had refused to marry him. Therefore he said, incessantly, in the language of Job, "I do well to be angry." The rubber tires revolved more slowly as his eye turned from the wayside to the smiling hills. The corn ears were sheathed in silvery yellow, but the afternoon sun jeweled the green pastures, fresh as in May (for rain had fallen in the morning), and maples, oaks and elms blended exquisite gradations of color and shade here and there among the open fields. Long rows of poplars recalled France to Somers, and he sighed. "These houses are all comfortable and all ugly," thought the artist. "I never saw anything less picturesque. The life hasn't even the dismal interest of poverty and revolt, for they are all beastly prosperous; and one of the farmers has offered me a hundred dollars and my expenses to come here and make a pastel of his wife. And I have taken the offer, because I want to pay my board bill and buy a second-hand bicycle. The chances are he is after something like a colored photograph, something slick and smooth, and every hair painted—oh, Lord!

But I *have* to have the money; and I won't
sign the cursed thing! What does he want
it for, though? I wonder, did *he* ever know
love's young dream? Dream? It's all a
dream—a mirage of the senses or the fancy.
Confound it! why need I be harking back
to it? I must be near his house. House
near the corner, they said, where the roads
cross—maybe this is it. Ugh! how it jumps
at the eyes!"

The house before him was yellow, with
pea green blinds; the great barns were In-
dian red; and a white fence glittered in
front of an old fashioned garden ariot with
scarlet salvias and crimson coxcomb. Two
men were talking, hidden to the waist by a
thicket of marigolds, out of which the sun
struck orange spangles. One of the men
smote the palm of his left hand with his
right fist as he talked—not vehemently, but
with a dogged air. His checked shirt and
brown overalls were as coarse and soiled as
the other man's, yet even a stranger could
perceive that he was the master. There
was a composure about the rugged gray
face, a look of control and care, that belongs

to the ruler, whether of large affairs or small.

He made an end of the talk by turning on his heel, whereupon the other flung an ugly word after the sturdy old back, and slunk off. At the gate he was joined by a companion. They passed Somers, who caught a single sentence: "Nit. I told you he wouldn't give no more. He's close as the bark of a tree."

Somers wheeled by, up to the gate and the old man, who was now leaning on the fence. He asked where Mr. Gates lived.

"Here," said the old man, not removing his elbows from the fence bar.

"And may I ask, are you Mr. Gates?" said Somers, bringing his wheel to a halt, with one foot on the curb stone.

"Yes, sir. But if you're the young man was round selling *Mother, Home and Heaven*, and going to call again to see if we liked it, we don't want it; you needn't git off. My wife can't read, and I'm taking a Chicago paper now, and ain't got any time."

Somers smiled and dismounted. "I'm not selling anything but pictures," said he, "and I believe you want me to make one for you."

"Are you Mr. Somers? F. J. S.?" cried the farmer, his face lightening in a surprising manner. "Well, I'm glad to see you, sir. My wife said you'd come this afternoon, and I wouldn't believe her; I'm always caught when I don't believe my wife. Come right in. Oh, got your tools with you?"

Somers having released his hand from a mighty grasp, was unstrapping a package on the under side of his saddle.

"I see. Handy little fixing. Ever in Ioway before?"

"Never," said Somers.

"Finest corn state in the Union; and second in production of flax. And lowest percentage of illiteracy. Hope they treated you well in town."

"Very well indeed, thank you."

"Generally do treat strangers well. We try to, anyhow. What do you think of our city?"

"Very pretty town."

"I'm glad you like it. Say, can't you

stay over night here and let me drive you round a little? We've got some of the prettiest brick pavements in the country, and our system of water works can't be beat; and the largest arsenal in the world is on the island——"

"You are awfully good," protested Somers deceitfully, "but I must leave for Chicago to-night; I'm not a free man, you know. The paper——"

"Say! that paper is smart enough. I like it. I took it jest to please my wife, so's to have something to read her in the evenings, and now I'd be lost without it. The man that writes them editorials, I tell you he's sound on the money question; he rakes them well. But I don't know but the best thing yet is your picters. You know that Columbia?"

Somers nodded, and put the released portfolio under his arm, awaiting his host's pleasure.

"Well, the minnit I saw that drawing— the first one—I said, 'Mother, if that feller had you to set to him, he wouldn't have made it much more like.' About the same height, too, only fatter ; but so like the way she looked when we was courting, it give me a start. I 've been seeking somebody to paint a picter for me of her for a long spell. The minnit I seen that, I says, 'There's my man.' I drawed the money out of bank this morning; it 's all ready. Guess you best take your bike along. Come right in and set down, and I 'll git you a glass of buttermilk off the ice. We churned to-day. Paper says that you wheelmen are great on buttermilk."

He guided Somers into the house, and into a room so dark that he stumbled.

"There 's the sofy ; set down," said Gates, who seemed full of hospitable cheer. "I 'll git a blind open. Girl's gone to the fair, and mother 's setting out on the back piazza, listening to the noises on the road. She 's all ready. Make yourself to home. Pastel like them picters on the wall 's what I want. My daughter done them." His tone changed on the last sentence, but Somers did not notice it; he was drinking in the details of the room to describe them after-ward to his sympathizing friends in Chicago. He smiled vaguely; he said, "Yes, certainly"; and his host went away, well content.

"What a chamber of horrors!" he thought; "and one can see he is proud of it." The carpet was soft to the foot, covered with a jungle of flowers and green leaves—the pattern of carpet which fashion leaves behind for disappointed salesmen to mark lower and lower, until it shall be pushed into the ranks of shop worn bargains. The cheap paper on the wall was delicately tinted, but this boon plainly came from the designers, and not the taste of the buyer, since there was a simply terrible chair that swayed by machinery, and had four brilliant hues of plush to vex the eye, besides a paroxysm of embroidery and lace, to which was still attached the red badge of courage of the county fair. More embroidery figured on the cabinet organ and two tables, and another red ticket peeped coyly from under the ornate frame of a pastel landscape displaying every natural beauty — forest, mountain, sunlit lake, and meadow — at their bluest and greenest.

There were three other pictures in the room — two very large colored photographs, one of a lad of twelve, the other of a pretty girl who might be sixteen, in a white gown, with a roll of parchment in her hand tied with a blue ribbon; and the photograph of a cross of flowers.

The girl's dark, wistful, timid eyes seemed to follow the young artist as he walked about the room. They appealed to him. "Poor little girl," he thought, "to have to live here!" Then he heard a dragging footfall, and there entered the mistress of the house. She was a tall woman who stooped. Her hair was gray and scanty, and so ill arranged on the top of her head that the mournful tonsure of age showed under the false gray braid. She was thin with the gaunt thinness of years and toil, not the poetic, appealing slenderness of youth. She had attired herself for the picture in a black silken gown, sparkling with jet that tinkled as she moved; the harsh, black, bristling line at the neck defined her withered throat brutally. Yet Somers's sneer was transient. He was struck by two things — the woman was blind; and she had once worn a face like that of the pretty girl — not her face, but a face like it. With a sensation of pity, he recalled Andrew Lang's verses; inaudibly, while she greeted him, he was repeating:

> "Who watches day by day
> The dust of time that stains her,
> The griefs that leave her gray,
> The flesh that still enchains her,
> Whose grace hath passed away."

Her eyes were closed, but she came straight toward him, holding out her hand. It was her left hand that was extended; her right closed over the top of a cane, and this added to the impression of decrepitude conveyed by her whole presence. She spoke in a gentle, monotonous, pleasant voice. "I guess this is Mr. Somers, the artist. I feel — we feel very glad to have the honor of meeting you, sir."

No one had ever felt honored to meet Somers before. He thought how much refinement and sadness were in a blind woman's face. In his most deferential manner he proffered her a chair. "I presume I am to paint you, madam," he said.

She blushed faintly. "Ain't it rediculous?" she apologized. "But Mr. Gates will have it. He has been at me to have somebody paint a picture of me ever since I had my photograph taken. It was a big picture, and most folks said it was real good, though not flattering; but he wouldn't hang it. He took it off, and I don't know what he did do to it. 'I want a real artist to paint you, mother,' he said. I guess if Kitty had lived she 'd have suited him, though she was all for landscape; never did much figures. You noticed her work in this room, ain't you?—on the table and chair and organ—art needle-work. Kitty could do anything. She took six prizes at the county fair; two of 'em come in after she was in her last sickness. She was so pleased she had the picture—that 's the picture right above the sofy; it 's a pastel —and the tidy—I mean the art needlework—put on her bed, and she looked at them the longest while. Her pa would never let the tickets be took off." She reached forth her hand to the chair near her and felt the ticket, stroking it absently, her chin quivering a little, while her lips smiled. "Mr. Gates was thinking," she said, "that maybe you'd paint a head of me — pastel like that landscape — that's why he likes pastel so. And he was thinking if — if maybe — my eyes was jest like Kitty's when we were married — if you would put in eyes, he would be awful much obliged, and be willing to pay extra, if necessary. Would it be hard?"

Somers dissembled a great dismay. "Certainly not," said he, rather dryly; and he was ashamed of himself, at the sensitive flutter in the old features.

"Of course I know," she said, in a different tone than she had used before — "I understand how comical it must seem to a young man to have to draw an old woman's picture; but it ain't comical to my husband. He wants it very much. He's the kindest man that ever lived, to me, caring for me all the time. He got me that organ — me that can't play a note, and never could — just because I love to hear music, and sometimes, if we have an instrument, the neighbors will come in, especially Hattie Knight, who used to know Kitty, and is a splendid performer; she comes and plays and sings. It is a comfort to me. And though I guess you young folks can't understand it, it will be a comfort to him to have a picture of me. I mistrusted you 'd be thinking it comical, and I hurried to come in and speak to you, lest, not meaning anything, you might, jest by chance, let fall something might hurt his feelings — like you thought it queer, or some sech thing. And he thinks so much of you, and having you here, that I couldn't bear there 'd be any mistake."

"Surely it is the most natural thing in the world he should want a portrait of you," interrupted Somers, hastily.

"Yes, it is," she answered, in her mild, even tones, "but it mightn't seem so to young folks. Young folks think they know all there is about loving. And it is very sweet and nice to enjoy things together; and you don't hardly seem to be in the world at all when you 're courting, your feet and your heart feel so light. But they don't know what it is to need each other. It 's when folks suffer together that they find out what loving is. I never knew what I felt toward my husband till I lost my first baby; and I 'd wake up in the night and there 'd be no cradle to rock — and he 'd comfort me. Do you see that picture under the photograph of the cross?"

"He 's a pretty boy," said Somers.

"Yes, sir. He was drownded in the river. A lot of boys in playing, you know, and one got too far, and Eddy, he swum out to help him. And he clumb up on Eddy, and the man on shore didn't git there in time. He was a real good boy, and liked to play home with me 'most as well as with the boys; and he 'd tell me the things he was going to get me. He was the greatest hand to make up stories of what he would do. But only in fun; he never told us a lie in his life — and it come hard sometimes for him to own up, for he was mis*chiev*ous. Father was proud as he could be of him, though he wouldn't let on. He was real bright, too; second in his class. I always felt he ought to have been head, but teacher said behavior counted, too, and Eddy *was* mis*chiev*ous. That cross was what his schoolmates sent; and teacher she cried when she told me how hard Eddy was trying to remember and mind and win the prize, to please his pa. Father and I went through that together. And we had to change all the things we used to talk of together, because Eddy was always in them; and we had to try not to let each other see how our hearts were breaking, and not shadder Kitty's life by letting her see how we missed him. Only once father broke down; it was when he give Kitty Eddy's colt." She stopped, for she could not go on.

"Don't — don't distress yourself," Somers begged, lamely. His cheeks were hot.

"It don't distress me," she answered, "only jest for the minnit; I'm always thinking of Eddy, and of Kitty, too. Sometimes I think it was harder for father when his girl went than anything else. And then my blindness and my rheumatism come; and it seemed like he was trying to make up to me for the daughter and the son I'd lost, and be all to once to me. He has been, too. And do you think that two old people that have grown old together, like us, and have been through losses like that — do you think they ain't drawed closer and kinder and tenderer to each other, like the Lord to His Church? Why, I'm plain and old and blind and crooked — but *he don't know it*. Now, do you understand?"

"Yes," said Somers, "I understand."

"And you'll please excuse me for speaking so free; it was only so father's feelings shouldn't git hurt by noticing maybe a look like you wanted to laugh."

"God knows I don't want to laugh," Somers burst in. "But I'm glad you spoke. It — it will be a better picture. Now may I ask you something? I want you to let me dress you — I mean put something about your neck, soft and white; and then I want to make two sketches of you — one, as Mr. Gates wishes, the head alone; the other, of you sitting in the rustic chair outside."

"But — she looked troubled — "it will be so expensive; and *I* know it will be foolish. If you'd jest the same —— "

"But I shouldn't; I want to do it. And it will not cost you anything. A hundred dollars will repay me well enough. I wish —I truly wish I could afford to do it all for nothing."

She gasped. "A hundred dollars! Oh, it ain't right! That was why he wouldn't buy the new buggy. And jest for a picture of me." But suddenly she flushed like a girl, and smiled.

At this instant the old man, immaculate in his heavy black suit and glossy white shirt, appeared in the doorway, bearing a tray.

"Father," said she, "do you mean to tell me you are going to pay a hundred dollars jest for a picture of *me?*"

"Well, mother, you know there's no fool like an old fool," he replied, jocosely; but when the old wife turned her sightless face toward the old husband's voice, and he looked at her, Somers bowed his head.

He spent the afternoon over his sketches. Riding away in the twilight, he knew that he had done better work than he had ever done in his life, slight as its form might be;

nevertheless, he was not thinking of his work, he was not thinking of himself at all. He was trying to shape his own vague perception that the show of dainty thinking and the pomp of refinement are in truth amiable and lovely things, yet are they no more than the husks of life; not only under them, but under ungracious and sordid conditions, may be the human semblance of that "beauty most ancient, beauty most new," that the old saint found too late. He felt the elusive presence of something in love higher than his youthful dream; stronger than passion, fairer than delight. To this commonplace man and woman had come the deepest gift of life.

"A dream?" he murmured; "yes, perhaps; but he has captured it." And he sang:

> " In dreams she grows not older,
>   The land of dreams among,
> Though all the world wax colder,
>   Though all the songs be sung;
> In dreams shall he behold her,
>   Still fair and kind and young."